D0859258

THE
RAMAYANA

Dedicated to

SHANKAR

in memory of his affection

THE RAMAYANA

Rendered by C.G.R. Kurup
Illustrated by B.G. Varma

Children's Book Trust, New Delhi

EDITED BY GEETA MENON

Text typeset in 13/17 pt. Centurion Old

© by CBT 2002
Reprinted 2003 (twice), 2005.

ISBN 81-7011-926-X

Published by Children's Book Trust, Nehru House, 4 Bahadur Shah Zafar Marg,
New Delhi-110002 and printed at its Indraprastha Press. Ph: 23316970-74
Fax: 23721090 e-mail: cbtnd@vsnl.com Website: www.childrensbooktrust.com

CONTENTS

Siva said to Parvathi: "The invocation of Rama's name is equal to the recital of the thousand names of Vishnu."

BALA KANDA
Heroic Princes

Ascetic Valmiki entreated sage Narada: "Who among men is perfect in form and conduct, prowess and resolve? Pray, answer me."

Narada replied: "Such a one is Rama. He is full of glory. He is illustrious in every sense."

The sage narrated Rama's story, concluding with the benediction that those who listened to the saga would be purified in mind and would achieve inner calm and beatitude.

Valmiki, after a while, repaired to the bank of the river Tamasa, not far from the holy Ganga, and bathed in its waters that flowed 'transparent as the mind of a righteous man'. So cleansed, he sauntered in the forest. Perceiving a pair of cranes moving about, hardly parting from each other and in mutual caress, Valmiki gazed in awe of the life-spirit. The sight filled his mind with joy. As he watched, a nishada (wild hunter), instinct with elation of killing, struck down with his arrow one of the mithuna (pair). It fell to the ground mortally hurt and bleeding all over. The deprived female, inflamed with passion and parted from her mate, gave out a deep wail. It filled Valmiki's heart with pity, which overflowed into a spontaneous lament:

maa nishada pratishtham tvamagamah saswateeh samaah
  yat krounchamithunaadekamavadheeh kamamohitam

(May you not have peace of mind for endless years, O, fowler, since you killed one of the pair of cranes, infatuated with passion!)

Valmiki remained in reverie over the incident.

God Brahma appeared before the sage and urged him, "O, jewel among seers, tell the story of Rama as heard by you from the lips of Narada. Every account known or unknown of Rama will reveal itself to you."

7

After God Brahma departed, the sage by virtue of his yogic power recollected the story of Rama, with every detail.

Valmiki composed the epic in the same poetic measure in seven kandas (divisions), namely, Bala Kanda, Ayodhya Kanda, Aranya Kanda, Kishkindha Kanda, Sundara Kanda, Yuddha Kanda and Uttara Kanda.

*   *   *

Vaivaswata Manu was the founder of a line of powerful kings who ruled as sovereigns of the earth. The lineage descending through his eldest son, Ikshwaku, included, among others, Trisanku, Sagara, Ansuman, Dilipa, Bhagiratha, Kakutastha, Raghu, Ambarisha, Nahusha, Yayati, and Aja, who was Dasaratha's father. King Bhagiratha was celebrated for his prodigious feat of bringing down the Ganga to the earth.

Dasaratha ruled from the kingdom of Kosala. It lay along the bank of the Sarayu river. Affluent and rich, it had its capital in Ayodhya (lit. unassailable). The city was built by Vaivaswata Manu. It was well-planned, with highways, gardens, orchards, mansions, gateways, markets, and halls made resonant with dance and music.

Dasaratha was a renowned king. He was an 'ati-ratha', a superb car-hero who could fight alone a number of 'maharathas' (car-warriors) defending himself, his charioteer and horses. Devoted to virtue, and possessing self-control, he had the qualities of a royal sage. Engaged in creating prosperity for his people, he ably protected the kingdom. His rule had 'kirti'(renown). His subjects by dint of their hard work, contentment, discipline and knowledge, remained happy and industrious—'yatha raja thatha praja' (like king, like his subjects).

The king had sagacious ministers, who were Dhrishti, Jayanta, Vijaya, Surashtra, Rashtravardhana, Akopa, Dharmapala, Arthavit and Sumantra. Vasishta and Vamadeva, who were great seers, were his family priests. The counsellors, among others, included Suyajna, Jabali, Markandeya and Katyayana.

The ministers were learned, well-versed in the use of weapons, vigilant and wise. They followed the precepts of political science. They were experts in administration and management of the state. Seasoned in every respect, they spoke kindly and with a smile on their lips. Learning made them polite and courteous.

Assisted by such ministers, seers, counsellors and the righteous, the king held sway over the earth.

Dasaratha had, as wives, Kausalya, Sumitra and Kaikeyi. The king performed the Aswamedha yaga (horse-sacrifice), and also the Putrakameshti ceremony (to pray for progeny).

Kausalya and Kaikeyi gave birth to a son each, and Sumitra two sons. All had auspicious bodily marks. The king was filled with supreme happiness. The entire Kosala rejoiced. Celestial musicians and artistes sang, danced and beat drums in jubilation. The streets got crowded with joyous people. The king bestowed presents and gave away riches.

At the naming ceremony, sage Vasishta bestowed on Kausalya's son, the eldest, the name of Rama (lit. beauteous, pleasing), Kaikeyi's son the name of Bharata (lit. maintained, controlled), Sumitra's sons, the names of Lakshmana (lit. with lustrous aspects) and Satrughna (lit. destroyer of foes).

The sage duly initiated the children into learning.

Rama shone with a rare radiance. An embodiment of virtues and amiable qualities, he was esteemed by all. Rama became a byword for auspiciousness ('abhirama').

The princes mastered the Vedas, and acquired knowledge of all branches of science and art. They became experts in archery and other modes of warfare. They exemplified heroism and prowess. Rama became a bowman with no equal. As the princes grew up, they remained devoted to their parents.

Lakshmana was deeply attached to Rama. The poet said: 'Lakshmana, rich in energy, was a second life, as it were, to Rama moving outside his body.' To Bharata, Satrughna was specially dear. They were fond of each other's proximity. The princes, with their accomplishments, were modest. Dasaratha and his consorts felt great satisfaction. So did all the citizens.

The princes concluded their studies.

The royal sage Viswamitra, who possessed unique power and merit, came to the palace. Dasaratha, who sat amidst his counsellors, heard the news with surprise and joy. He, together with the family priests, received the sage with due ceremony. He said: "O, great sage, I wonder what supreme desire of yours I can fulfil! Your coming makes me, my queens, and sons feel blessed."

Viswamitra said: "You are privileged to be advised by the wise sage Vasishta. I stand committed to a sacrificial performance. Two ogres capable of taking any form at will, along with others, attempt to hinder the observance and wreck its conclusion. These are notorious rakshasas (lit. night-rangers), Maricha and Subahu. Possessing wild might and subtle cunning, they defile the sacred altar with flesh and blood. Your son, Rama, has the ability to deal with them. O, king of kings, make over the lotus-eyed Rama to me for a period of ten days and nights."

Dasaratha, who heard the suggestion, remained senseless for a long while. Regaining consciousness, he spoke: "My Rama, beautiful and virtuous, is less than sixteen years old. He is yet to have the capacity to fight the rakshasas. If you are keen, take me, and my powerful army along. I shall personally engage the ogres. You ought not to ask for Rama. His absence is beyond endurance for me. My supreme affection binds him."

Viswamitra replied: "There is the rakshasa-king Ravana who is son of sage Visrava, progeny of rishi Pulastya born of the

11

mind of God Brahma. Ravana is half-brother of Kubera, lord of wealth, being the eldest son of Visrava. Ravana revels in wrong actions owing to a boon from God Brahma, namely, immunity from death at the hands of all except a human being. Possessing extraordinary strength, he oppresses the three worlds. Employed by Ravana, Maricha and Subahu obstruct my sacrifice."

Dasaratha observed, his words faltering: "Even the gods being no match for Ravana, Rama shall not contend with the notorious pair, Maricha and Subahu. It is sure to be perilous."

Viswamitra, who burnt with rage, said: "You are going back on your offer, unworthy of a scion of the Raghu race! This will be ruinous of its fame." As the sage was seized with fury, the earth shook. Fear gripped the gods.

Dreading the consequences, Vasishta intervened to tell the king: "You ought not to abandon righteousness. None can conquer Rama so long as he is guarded by Viswamitra, who is a repository of intense asceticism. He possesses divine missiles of war and is capable of evolving new ones. Though able to punish the rakshasas himself, he wants to do good to your son, hence his request. He knows every aspect of dharma (righteousness). Therefore, send him, with your blessing."

So pacified and assured, Dasaratha called Rama and Lakshmana and committed them to the care of Viswamitra. The princes took the blessing of their father, mothers Kausalya and Sumitra, and the benediction of Vasishta. As Rama and Lakshmana walked by the side of the sage, the heavenly beings showered flowers on them.

Having walked along the Sarayu river, the sage administered to the princes the spells 'bala' and 'atibala', which would keep them free from thirst and fatigue and loss of their comeliness. They spent the night on the bank of the river, sleeping on a bed of dry leaves.

At dawn, after observing the morning devotions, the party moved. They saw the Ganga, at its confluence with the Sarayu. Many hermitages stood on its banks. The party spent the night in a hermitage. The sage regaled them with delightful stories.

In the morning, Viswamitra and the brothers boarded a boat for crossing the river. Midstream, they heard the loud noise caused by the striking of waves. Rama enquired the cause of the tumult. The sage said, the Sarayu, which flowed from lake Manasa in the Himalaya, rushed to meet the Ganga, also called the Jahnavi. The latter stream (the Ganga) was drunk off by sage Jahnu, for its waters inundated his sacrificial ground; the river was released through his ears, hence its name Jahnavi. Rama and Lakshmana saluted the twin rivers. Reaching the south bank of the Ganga, they beheld an intense forest.

Viswamitra told the princes: "Tataka, a yaksha (semi-divine) woman, turned into an ogress under a curse, who dwells in the forest, has the might of a thousand elephants! Wife of Sunda, and mother of Maricha, she ravages the entire region, and is a source of terror to all. Tataka, who obstructs their path, should be destroyed. There should be no qualms in killing a woman who harasses living beings. A prince's duty is to protect. Unrighteous and impious, she should die. Therefore, O, Rama, shake off tenderness in performing your duty."

So enjoined, Rama wielded his bow, its twang making the quarters resound with the noise. Tataka, who got terribly enraged, rushed angrily in the direction from which the sound had emanated. Seeing her, Rama told Lakshmana: "The heart of the timorous will break at her sight. On the sage's advice, let me put an end to her prowess, thus preventing her from further devastation."

Tataka rushed to Rama, roaring and lifting her arms. Adept in conjuring tricks, she confused the princes by raising a huge

cloud of dust. She tried to cover them with a shower of rocks. Parrying, Rama sent a stream of shafts and cut off her arms. Lakshmana deprived her of her ears and sliced her nose. Assuming an enormous form, Tataka went out of sight. The princes were mystified, as her truncated form moved hither and thither unseen. Viswamitra cautioned Rama, who was prone to tenderness to a woman, not to delay her destruction. Thereupon, Rama used his skill in hitting a target not visible to the eye yet piercing it with the help of the sound. His arrows impeded her. Hit on her chest, Tataka charged forward impetuously, and fell. The gods were pleased and praised sage Viswamitra.

Twilight set in. The princes rested in the forest, in the company of the sage. Viswamitra, much gratified, and filled with deep affection, imparted to Rama the secret of all missiles. These included the Chakra, presided over by God Vishnu, the Sulavata presided by God Siva, the Brahmasira, and the Aisika employed through the medium of a reed, rush or stem of a grass. He gave Rama the maces, Modaki and Sikhari, the noose wielded by Kala (Time-spirit), the noose ruled by Lord Varuna, sea god, and the missile Sikhara presided over by fire god. The missile Mohana was called so, for it could stupefy the enemy. As the sage silently chanted the spells, the missiles appeared before Rama in their ethereal forms. The prince accepted them with a cheerful mind, desiring to them 'appear in my mind whenever I think of you'. The sage also taught him the mantras (spells) for recalling the missiles.

On entering Viswamitra's hermitage, Siddhashrama, the ascetics present paid homage to him. They offered hospitality to the princes. They requested Viswamitra to go through the ceremony of consecration for the sacrificial performance.

Rama and Lakshmana rested for the night. At dawn, they enquired about the time when the ogres Maricha and Subahu needed to be guarded against. Delighted, the hermits answered: "From this day, keep vigil for six days and nights continuously. We say this inasmuch as sage Viswamitra will observe silence during these days."

Rama and Lakshmana stood guard of the hallowed grove, armed with weapons. As the final day arrived, the air was filled with the recital of the sacred texts. The sacrificial fire blazed forth.

There arose a loud clamour in the sky. The demons, Maricha and Subahu manifested, like monsoon clouds, darkening the sky. They, along with their accomplices, attempted to rain torrents of blood and flesh. Seeing the malevolent ones in the sky, Rama, full of alertness and agility, fitted to his bow the most excellent and supremely effulgent missile presided over by Manu and hurled it angrily at the breast of Maricha. Hit by it, the demon was hoisted and flung in mid-ocean over a hundred yojanas (eight hundred miles). He lay senseless. Thereafter Rama invoked the missile presided over by fire god, and hurled it at the breast of Subahu. Pierced by it, the demon fell dead on the ground. Using the missile presided over by wind god, Rama scattered the rest of the demons.

Rama's heroic feat brought joy to the sages. The sacrifice concluded, sage Viswamitra, who stood accomplished of purpose, blessed Rama for his meritorious deed. The sage, along with Rama and Lakshmana, offered prayers to the evening twilight.

Having performed their tasks, Rama and Lakshmana spent the night in a cheerful mood, in the sacrificial hall. In the morning, they enquired if any further task awaited them. "O, most honoured sage, what injunction of yours should we carry out?"

Knowing the mind of Viswamitra, the sages announced that

Janaka, king of Mithila, was going to perform a most pious sacrifice. "O, princes, you should accompany us to the sacrifice. There you will see a bow, marvellous in its power and lustre. It was presented to Devarata, a former king of Mithila, by the gods, who had received it from God Siva. It remained worshipped and enshrined in the palace." The princes were thrilled to hear this.

Viswamitra set out on the journey with Rama and Lakshmana, accompanied by the other sages. They broke the journey on the bank of the Sone. Having reposed for the night, they crossed the river in the morning. Travelling a long way, they reached the Ganga. All rejoiced to see the legendary river. They bathed in its waters and propitiated the manes and gods with the offer of water. Rama desired to hear the story of the Ganga as it coursed through heaven and the earth.

Viswamitra narrated the story.

King Sagara, who ruled from Ayodhya, practised asceticism in the Himalaya along with his two wives, Kesini and Sumati. He practised penance for a hundred years. Sage Bhrigu, born of the mind of God Brahma, who was pleased, conferred a boon on Sagara for begetting sons and attaining unique fame in the world. "One wife of yours will bear you a son who will perpetuate your race while the other will give birth to sixty-thousand sons." To Kesini was born Asamanja, and to Sumati sixty-thousand sons. The valiant son of Asamanja, Ansuman, was beloved of the people.

Sagara undertook to perform a sacrifice. It took place in the region lying between the Himalaya and the Vindhya ranges, designated as Aryavarta. Ansuman accompanied the sacrificial horse. Lord Indra took away the horse. The king ordered his sixty-thousand sons to track out the thief. They excavated the earth in all directions. Under the digging of the mighty princes, the earth groaned. All the living beings, gods, demons and celestials cried in anguish. God Vishnu, who has the earth as his consort, assumed the form of sage Kapila and sought to support the earth. Splitting the earth to find the horse, the princes dug their way into rasatala, a region of beauty and splendour, where they saw sage Kapila, and also a horse. The princes rushed to the sage in frenzy of anger. Outraged, Kapila uttered in contempt the word 'hum'. The princes lay reduced to a heap of ashes.

On the orders of Sagara, Ansuman, who combined deep asceticism with prowess, set out in search of the horse. In rasatala he found the sons of Sagara, his uncles, lying reduced to ashes. He saw the sacrificial horse grazing on the pastures. Ansuman longed to offer water to the spirits of the princes but did not find it anywhere around.

Garuda, God Vishnu's mount, who appeared there, advised Ansuman that the waters of the sacred Ganga brought down from the Himalaya should wash the ashes of his uncles for salvation of their spirits. He was advised to take the sacrificial horse, in the meanwhile, for the completion of his grandfather's sacrifice. Ansuman accordingly returned, leading the horse. Sagara concluded his sacrifice. After a long rule, the king ascended to heaven.

Ansuman, who succeeded him, performed severe austerities to invoke the Ganga to come down. He passed away. His son Dilipa, who was full of piety, did not know how to bring the river to the terrestrial plane, his judgement having been clouded by sorrow.

Dilipa had a son, Bhagiratha, who was most conscientious in his duties.

Bhagiratha became not only a ruler but became a royal sage. Entrusting the governance of the kingdom to his ministers, he practised intense ascesis on a Himalayan summit praying for the descent of goddess Ganga to purify the spirits of his ancestors. With uplifted arms and subdued senses, he did his severe penance. A thousand years passed. God Brahma appeared before the high-souled king and granted his desire.

"Great is this ambition of yours," the Creator warned that none other than God Siva could stand the impetuosity of the Ganga as she descended from heaven. Bhagiratha prayed to God Siva, remaining standing on one toe, for a year. Propitiated, God Siva agreed to receive the Ganga.

As the divine river fell irresistibly, God Siva received her on his head. She lay a captive in his extensive, dense, matted hair. Through further austerities Bhagiratha pleased God Siva, who let the Ganga fall into the lake Bindusarovar in the Himalaya. Falling, the river split into seven streams. These became famed as Hladoni, Pavani, Nalini, running in an easterly direction, Suchaksu, Sita, Sindhu flowing in a westerly direction. The seventh one flowed following Bhagiratha who was mounted on a beautiful chariot, invested with unique splendour and piety. Hence the name Tripathaga (following a three-fold path) for the Ganga. She made the Jambudwipa (name for India) blessed.

The Ganga flowed swiftly, tortuously, now broadening, buffeted by her own waves, narrowing, falling into ravines, tossing high and dashing to the ground. The river shone bright on the earth, purifying everything in her course. As she flowed, the Ganga (Jahnavi) followed Bhagiratha and forced her way into rasatala. Her waters submerged the ashes of Sagara's sons and purified them of their sins. This consummated Bhagiratha's purpose, and hence the name Bhagirathi for the Ganga.

The exceptional glory of his forbear, Bhagiratha, as narrated by Viswamitra filled Rama's heart with joy.

It was evening, Rama and Lakshmana pondered over the story

during the whole night. In the morning, Rama said: "Most wonderful, O, sage, is this story told by you!"

Viswamitra, Rama and Lakshmana, and the host of rishis accompanying them ferried across the river and visited the city of Visala. King Sumati duly honoured them. They spent the night there.

They resumed their journey to Mithila. On the outskirts of the city, they saw a beautiful grove and in it an old, delightful yet desolate hermitage. This stirred Rama's curiosity, whereupon the sage told the rare story.

The hermitage remained under a curse. It belonged to the high-souled sage, Gautama, and his spouse Ahalya, who originally lived there. Discovering misconduct on the part of his spouse that occurred unwittingly on account of Lord Indra disguising himself as the sage and ravishing her, Gautama cursed her to dwell frozen until Rama's feet fell on her! On the advice of Viswamitra, Rama and Lakshmana entered the hermitage.

Ahalya, thus purified, and reaching the end of her curse which lasted for a very long time, recovered her glorious form. Rama accepted her hospitality. Gautama returned to his hermitage and resumed his austerities.

Viswamitra, Rama and Lakshmana, and the sages reached Mithila and halted at a secluded spot. Hearing of their arrival, king Janaka, who had true humility, went forth all at once to meet them. Satananda, his family priest, and other ascetics did homage to Viswamitra. The king was struck by the dignity of the princes who looked like a pair of gods. He enquired who they were.

Viswamitra introduced them—sons of emperor Dasaratha. He told about their journey from Ayodhya, the heroic deed of the killing of Tataka by the princes, their protection of his sacrifice, and the liberation of Ahalya. They were visiting Mithila to look at the great bow during the king's sacrifice.

Kings and mighty warriors besieged Mithila to test their strength.

On the orders of the king, five thousand strong men propelled the chest containing the bow, mounted on eight wheels. Janaka said: "This bow adorned with sandal paste and flowers is worshipped by the line of kings, the Janakas. Even gods were unable to string it."

Viswamitra said: "Child Rama, behold the bow."

Viewing the bow uncased, Rama said: "I shall hold with my hand this excellent heavenly bow and shall try to toss it on my palms and even to bend it."

Rama seized the bow at the middle and strung it as if in sport as many thousands of men stood looking on and, setting the string to it, he bent it, and lo, the bow broke into two in the middle! A noise like a crash of thunder issued from it. Earth trembled; men, stunned, toppled down.

The king addressed Viswamitra: "The feat is most marvellous, Rama who achieved it shall have my dear daughter Sita (lit. plough furrow; one recovered from furrow/field). My pledge that Sita can be won only through valour stands redeemed. Having secured Rama as her husband she will fetch renown to the race of the Janakas."

With the consent of Viswamitra, Janaka despatched his select counsellors to emperor Dasaratha in Ayodhya. Ushered into the court, they gave king Janaka's message in polite language: "The celebrated daughter of mine, Sita, has been decisively won by your beloved son, Rama, who broke the superb heavenly bow of God Siva! She remains to be given away by me to the exalted hero. O, great king, arrive and be pleased to see Rama and Lakshmana."

Dasaratha sought the advice of Vasishta and Vamadeva. They approved the proposed alliance. Dasaratha instructed Sumantra

to send ahead to Mithila officers taking with them abundant riches, as also the army consisting of its four limbs—the horses, the chariots, the elephants and the infantry. Priests and sages, Vasishta, Vamadeva, Jabali, Markandeya, as also others, should proceed to Mithila.

Dasaratha started on his journey to Mithila the next day. Travelling in his chariot for four days, Dasaratha reached the Videha territory (hence Vaidehi for Sita).

On seeing Dasaratha, king Janaka experienced much joy. "Welcome is your advent, O, noble sovereign! On conclusion of the (bow) sacrifice tomorrow, you ought to celebrate the wedding with the help of the foremost of sages, Vasishta." Dasaratha replied, "We shall do as you bid us." Rama and Lakshmana touched their father's feet. They rejoiced in the company of Bharata and Satrughna.

Concluding the rites connected with the sacrifice, Janaka summoned his younger brother Kusadhwaja, from the city of Sankasya. He arrived. He had two daughters, Mandavi and Srutakirti.

Dasaratha visited the king, taking with him his preceptors and counsellors. Thereafter, Vasishta, with the approval of Dasaratha and sage Viswamitra narrated the noble lineage of Dasaratha from Vaivaswata Manu.

Janaka for his part narrated his genealogy. The race descended from Nimi, a most pious king. His son was Mithi, whose son was Janaka, the first ruler bearing the title. Many righteous and powerful kings descended in the line. From the royal sage Swarnaroma was born the high-souled Hraswaroma. "I was born to him, and my younger brother, Kusadhwaja. I offer most delightfully my two daughters in marriage, Sita for Rama and Urmila for Lakshmana."

Sage Viswamitra, accompanied by Vasishta, addressed Janaka:

"The royal houses of Ikshwaku and Videha are inconceivably great and immeasurably esteemed. The sacred alliance going to be contracted is well-matched, for Sita and Urmila are becoming spouses for Rama and Lakshmana. There is more to be said. We sue, as wives to prince Bharata and Satrughna, your brother's daughters, Mandavi and Srutakirti. Through the marriages of these pairs let both the royal houses be bound."

Janaka replied: "Let it be so; I consider my pedigree blessed, for the advice came from two most exalted sages. Let the marriages take place on the same day. A supreme merit has been conferred upon me." King Dasaratha agreed to the alliances as proposed.

Bharata's maternal uncle, Yudhajit, Kaikeyi's brother, and son of the Kekaya king, Aswapati, arrived. King Dasaratha honoured him with the utmost attention.

On the suggestion of Janaka, Dasaratha got performed the ceremonies samvartana (indicating conclusion of studies in respect of his sons) and nadisraddha (to propitiate departed ancestors).

In the morning on the wedding day, Dasaratha and his sons dressed in festive attire arrived at the marriage pavilion, placing Vasishta and other honoured sages at their head. Vasishta spoke to Janaka: "Perform the noble rights pertaining to the weddings, and discharge your sacred obligation to king Dasaratha." Janaka requested Vasishta: "Along with the other sages, O, pious seer, conduct the nuptial ceremony of Rama, to the delight of the world."

Vasishta erected the altar, decorated it with sandal paste, flowers, gold, jars of variegated colours containing sprouts, vessels containing incense, vessels filled with parched grains of paddy, as also grains of unbroken rice dyed with turmeric. The altar was bestrewn with the darbha (sacrificial) grass.

Vasishta raised the fire and poured oblations into it, with the recitation of the holy texts.

Janaka took Sita, adorned with many kinds of jewels, seated her before the sacred fire opposite Rama. He addressed Rama, "Take Sita's hand in your own and accept her as your own. She will remain devoted to you, and will ever follow you as a shadow." Rama did as asked. The marriage was consecrated solemnly. The celestials sounded kettle drums. The gods rained an abundant shower of flowers, exclaiming: "Well done!"

Likewise Janaka gave Urmila to Lakshmana, Mandavi to Bharata, and Srutakirti to Satrughna. As the princes and their brides went through the ceremonies prescribed by the scriptures, celestial nymphs danced and gandharvas (musicians) sang. Flowers rained.

The ceremonies over, the princes and their spouses retired to their palaces. In the morning sage Viswamitra, taking leave of the kings, left for his hermitage.

Seeking permission from Janaka, Dasaratha and his sons and their consorts prepared themselves to leave for Ayodhya. Janaka gave a rich dowry of cows, carpets, garments, elephants, horses, plenty of silver, gold, pearls and coral beads. Having received them, Dasaratha, his sons, and their spouses departed, duly accompanied by many sages, the royal entourage and army.

As the party proceeded, bad omens occurred. Birds began to cry fearfully. Frightened deer in numbers crossed the path. Dasaratha's mind was filled with anxiety. A tempest set in, shaking the globe. The sun got enveloped in darkness, the directions remained hidden covered all over with dust, and the army stood dumbfounded. In the dreadful darkness, Dasaratha discovered Parasurama, son of sage Jamadagni, born in the race of Bhrigu (hence Bhargava) and destroyer of the Kshatriya kings. He wore matted locks formed into a coil at the crown,

blazing with effulgence, wielding an axe in one hand, and a bow and shaft flashing like lightning in the other. Seeing the sage of awesome aspect, all exclaimed 'Rama, O, Rama'.

Parasurama addressed Rama: "Valiant prince! Your prowess in splitting the bow of God Siva is marvellous, indeed! It cannot be conceived. Hearing of it, I have arrived, carrying another sacred bow, which I received from my father. Draw it to its full length, fit an arrow to it and demonstrate your strength. Having shown your prowess, meet me in a single combat, which will bring you credit."

The challenge made Dasaratha scared. He spoke: "Having given up your anger towards the Kshatriyas, and turned calm and ascetic, you ought to give assurance of safety to my young sons." Turning a deaf ear to the entreaty, Parasurama said to Rama: "This bow, as the one which you broke, was made by Viswakarma. It is hard to prevail against, being that of God Vishnu. It was bestowed on my father who, having given up the use of arms, had no use for it. Karthaveerarjuna, called Sahasrabahu because of his thousand arms, caused my father's death. In retaliation for the cruel deed, I for my part uprooted the Kshatriyas twentyone times out of indignation. I took up my abode in mount Mahendra for austerities. Hearing of your snapping of God Siva's bow, I arrived here. Accept my challenge as a true warrior."

Dasaratha remained perplexed.

Rama, out of regard for his father, spoke to the sage: "I have heard of your harsh revenge. You hold me in contempt, being a Kshatriya devoted to his duty. I am chary of speech, in reverence for you, as if lacking in virility. O, scion of Bhrigu, witness my prowess today."

The sages and ascetics emerged from their abodes, and the celestials and the gods with the Creator at their head in the aerial cars assembled to witness the unique encounter. They looked stunned at the sight of Rama's heroism.

Rama seized, in sport yet with modesty, God Vishnu's bow and the arrow from Parasurama. Stringing the bow swiftly, he fitted the arrow to it, and said, "You are worthy of respect to me as a holy Brahmana; I respect you for the merit you have earned and your kinship with sage Viswamitra (who was his father's maternal uncle). Therefore, I dare not hurl at you this arrow of God Vishnu which, capable of crushing the might as well as the pride of the adversary by its power, never goes without hitting its target. In the alternative, it could destroy the ethereal glory earned through your austerities."

So addressed, Parasurama who looked with wonder at Rama spoke gently: "O, Rama, I conclude you to be no less than the imperishable Vishnu, who is the lord of the three worlds. Your feat is therefore no shame to me. Discharge your arrow targeting the merit of my austerities."

The arrow released by Rama deprived Parasurama of his spiritual supremacy. As the gods and the hosts of rishis applauded, Bhargava walked clockwise round Rama, who stood with the uplifted bow, and retired in serene calm with a sense of fulfilment to mount Mahendra to resume his penance.

Parasurama having departed, Rama entrusted God Vishnu's bow to Lord Varuna.

Dasaratha was freed from the trauma. He thought his son as well as himself reborn on the occasion! He embraced Rama. The king was full of joy witnessing Rama's prowess in the encounter and urged his army forward. Dasaratha, his sons, daughters-in-law, and entourage finally entered Ayodhya, which had been decorated by the joyous citizens who thronged its streets. They were welcomed by the people.

The queens busied themselves with the ceremonious reception to their daughters-in-law. They took Sita and the other brides into the gynaeceum, and got them to offer worship in the temples where they received benedictions. They made oblations to the sacred fire. Thereafter the princesses lived happily with their husbands.

A little time later, Dasaratha sent Bharata and Satrughna to Kekaya in the company of Yudhajit.

Rama and Lakshmana remained steadfast in the service of their father. Rama attended to the causes which were conducive to the people's interests.

Rama enjoyed life with Sita. Her manifold virtues and her comeliness became dear to Rama. She shed sweetness and lustre. Rama exuding excellence and nobility got enthroned in Sita's heart. The poet said that Sita, who with her beauty and exquisite tenderness shone like a goddess, could vividly read even thoughts in the innermost recess of Rama's heart. Rama shone like God Vishnu with Goddess Lakshmi beside him.

AYODHYA KANDA

Into Exile

King Dasaratha held his sons dearly. Rama, being richly endowed, gave him ecstatic joy. Tranquil of mind, he spoke softly and was clear in his utterances. He did not retort when spoken to harshly. He felt gratified with a single good turn rendered, whereas repeated wrongs did not perturb him for the reason he gained control over his self. He conversed with men of piety and enlightenment. He was affable, and not proud in spite of his extraordinary prowess. Respect for elders remained a deep trait in him. He loved the people. He was unique in his quality of compassion. He symbolised abhaya (freedom from fear; a refuge from fear). Rama could be likened only to Rama.

Ever intent on what was worthy of his lineage, Rama's mind was set on his duty as a Kshatriya.

Imbued with such superb qualities, Rama grew to be adored by the king's subjects. Instructed by teachers mellowed in wisdom, he imbibed liberal principles and fostered secular interests. Righteous conduct was basic to his nature which did not however alienate him from material enjoyment and prosperity. He possessed rare skill in ways of management, which included handling of funds and expending of money as laid down by the sastras (ancient texts). A good judge of men, he was adept in meting out punishments and bestowing favours according to the norms of equity. He mastered the various departments of knowledge which made him a connoisseur of the aesthetic arts intended to give delight to oneself.

Apart from being the foremost of those who perfected archery, he was thorough in all aspects of warfare, and could not be overpowered in an encounter by man, god or demon in rage. He was unconquerable.

Seeing Rama so accomplished, and beloved of his subjects, Dasaratha thought, 'commiserating all created beings, Rama truly seeks the advancement of all, and should therefore succeed him to the throne during his own lifetime'. This supreme idea revolved in his mind ever. He proposed to install Rama as prince regent and consulted his ministers. He caused to be summoned to the assembly the prominent citizens of various cities, as also rulers of the different regions of the country.

Since no time was to be lost, Dasaratha did not convey his intentions to the Kekaya king or king Janaka. He was certain that the two rulers would receive the news of the event duly with delight.

Addressing the assembly, Dasaratha announced his intention. "Rama possessing unique splendour will become your worthy protector, and protector of the whole earth." The kings and others present applauded the idea heartily: "Many benignant qualities inhere in your son, who, apart from his superhuman heroism, is full of amiability, is free from arrogance and is comforting, polite of speech, and rich in self-discipline. Earth seeks Rama as its master. In our interest, you ought to install Rama as prince regent."

Dasaratha spoke to Vasishta, Vamadeva and other counsellors. "The present is the sacred month of Chaitra (nearly corresponding to March) when the woodlands are adorned with blossoms. Let everything be got ready for the ceremony."

Preparations were to begin on sunrise the next day with the performance of swasti-vachana, a religious rite preparatory to a solemn observance.

On the king's orders, Sumantra brought Rama to his presence. He said, "All the people are gratified by you through your excellence. Therefore, you are to accept the office of prince regent tomorrow, at the auspicious time."

The close friends and admirers of Rama, who got the news, conveyed it to Kausalya.

Rama went to his mother's apartments. He found her devoted to the worship of her chosen deity and waited upon by Sumitra and Lakshmana praying for him. Rama said, "Mother, I have been entrusted by father with the duty of ruling over the people. My installation is to take place tomorrow. Sita and I need to keep a fast tonight as enjoined by father." Sita was sent for to join them. Kausalya, shedding tears of joy, said, "My child, my prayers to God Narayana have not gone in vain." Rama turned to Lakshmana and said, "Rule you beneficially over this earth with me. This fortune has come to you who are my second life."

In the morning, the citizens began to decorate the city with flags and buntings on the temples, streets, trees, sacrificial sites, residences and assembly halls. The dancers danced and the musicians sang to the delight of the people, who assembled welcoming the news of the installation of Rama. Boys played in joy. Trees shone with lights on their boughs. The villagers poured into the city from all directions in order to witness the ceremony.

The city was thus in a festal mood. Kausalya distributed gifts to the Brahmanas and others.

Manthara, a hunchback, who was a trusted servant of Kaikeyi, beheld the preparations as she had by chance climbed to the roof of the palace. Coming to hear of the forthcoming installation of Rama as prince regent, she felt outraged!

Filled with indignation, Manthara rushed down and, approaching Kaikeyi even while she was reposing in bed, told her of the imminent event. Receiving the wonderful news, Kaikeyi gifted Manthara a precious jewel. The news was 'nectar-like' to her! Kaikeyi eulogized Rama, "As Bharata is worthy of praise, Rama is even more so. Nay, the latter does greater

service to me than to Kausalya. If the throne goes to Rama, it will be equally Bharata's, for Rama esteems his brothers."

Manthara said, "O, proud lady, I shudder to think of the danger to your son! You will with joined palms wait humbly like a servant on Kausalya."

Manthara pursued her vile logic for long. The venom rubbed in tirelessly started working, Kaikeyi shedding the inhibition of her love for Rama. She was puzzled. With a doleful sigh, she enquired how she was to achieve the purpose!

Manthara reminded her of the two boons which were given to her by Dasaratha for helping him in a critical situation in his war against the demons on behalf of the gods. She should demand the bestowing of the boons, namely, exile for Rama, and installation in his place of her son, using the preparations which were on. She warned: "No dam is built across a stream when its waters have flowed out! Therefore work your salvation."

Kaikeyi, who was shaken, reconciled herself to the logic.

She pondered. After casting off her ornaments, she entered the sulking chamber and threw herself on the bare floor. The stage was set for the perfidy.

Dasaratha was searching for Kaikeyi to break to her the happy news of the proposed installation of Rama. Going to the sulking chamber, he found her in utter distress! Not knowing the reason, the king, who was ever infatuated by her beauty and charm, cajoled her.

"If you make a vow to accomplish my desire, I shall reveal my mind," said Kaikeyi. The king declared, "I swear by Rama, the foremost among men, and by my other sons, that your bidding will be done." Kaikeyi articulated, "You would recall the two boons which you gave me while fighting the demons to help the devas. These should be granted now." Dasaratha avowed. Kaikeyi said, "One, Bharata should be installed prince regent

36

using the preparations made; two, Rama should go to the Dandaka forest, to live the life of a hermit for fourteen years."

Hearing the words, Dasaratha swooned. Recovering and distressed as a deer in front of a lioness, the king asked, "What wrong had been done to you by Rama, O, wretch? Rama ever served you as he does Kausalya. I touch your feet with my head. Let Bharata be installed; what for have you suggested exile of Rama?"

Kaikeyi said the king had his choice, either going back on his promises, or seeing her die the same day before his very eyes by drinking poison! Nothing short of either would satisfy her. She spoke no further, as the king waited. Left in the horrendous suspense on hearing the proposals, Dasaratha fell to the ground. Kaikeyi tormented him, and called him a 'brag'.

The king wailed as Kaikeyi continued to harass him. The night thus passed.

At dawn, Kaikeyi told the king he ought to summon Rama to act in order to honour his father's boons to her. She goaded Dasaratha to command the minister to fetch Rama.

The entrance to Rama's palace and the streets were crowded with people rejoicing over the event for which preparations were going on.

Rama had told Sita his proposed installation. Sita was filled with happiness. Rama left to meet his father through multitudes of happy citizens who had gathered. Reaching the palace, Rama went alone to the royal presence. Rama beheld his father seated on the couch, dejected and distressed, with a withered face. He bowed to his father and thereafter he laid himself low at Kaikeyi's feet. The afflicted king neither spoke nor looked at him being blinded by tears. Seeing his father a victim of grief, Rama in utter dismay thought to himself 'how does my father feel agonized in seeing me today?' Bowing with folded hands, Rama asked Kaikeyi the cause of his father's sorrow.

Kaikeyi with a heart grown hard as adamant said, "O, Rama, beware lest the king shall forsake truth. I have desired the two boons which your father had gifted me. I have sought that Bharata be installed prince regent. Secondly, wearing matted locks and the bark of trees, you should depart for the Dandaka forest to live there in exile for fourteen years. You should do your duty."

Hearing the words, Rama did not yield to grief in the least. He said, "Be pleased with me. Honouring my father's pledges, I shall give up the kingdom in favour of Bharata, who would be brought with swift speed for his installation. I shall proceed to the Dandaka forest." Overcome with sadness and sorrow, the king fell unconscious. Even as Rama lifted him with his hands,

Kaikeyi urged Rama to hasten to go to the forest. Rama addressed Kaikeyi, "Pursuing such a frivolous purpose, you caused sorrow to my father! O, princess of Kekaya, bear with me till I take leave of my mother, Kausalya, and win Sita's consent." Bowing at the feet of his father lying senseless, Rama departed. Lakshmana followed on his heels, highly enraged, his eyes filled with tears.

The poet said none around Rama noticed any change in his mood or countenance as he proceeded to Kausalya who had passed the night in religious observances, wishing well of her son. Rama said, "O, godly lady, what I am going to say will cause you agony. Father is installing Bharata as prince regent, I am to go in exile to live in the Dandaka forest for fourteen years."

Kausalya dropped to the ground. Rama lifted her up. She knew that in Rama's absence she would be despised even more by Kaikeyi.

Highly enraged, Lakshmana felt Rama should not accept the command of the king, which was ignoble. Kausalya listened intently, for separation from Rama was for her unthinkable. Rama consoled Kausalya. He told Lakshmana that in obeying his father he would only be following the path of his forbears. Indeed, righteousness was paramount in the world. "My father's command rooted in righteousness is supreme. Therefore, give up any unworthy thought, namely, my gaining the kingdom. Let my resolution be carried out. I shall go into exile, let there be no delay." Lakshmana remained silent in obedience to his brother. Rama and Lakshmana took leave of Kausalya.

Rama addressed Lakshmana: "Banish your anger with uncommon fortitude, for great merit lies in fulfilling our father's vow. Let not mother Kaikeyi be troubled by apprehension about our revolting attitude. Let us show the same zeal for going to the forest as we showed in preparing for the installation. Our parents' agony is sure to distress us. Therefore it is doubly unworthy." Lakshmana argued that their father's wish should be ignored as being unrighteous. "It is repellent to me." Rama, again admonishing Lakshmana, concluded by deciding to surrender to their father's wish. "For such is the path of the dutiful."

Finding Rama firm in his resolve, Kausalya pleaded she could go with him to the forest. Rama did not accept her suggestion, for being so abandoned his father would not survive. Her service lay with his father, for a woman, however noble and devoted to sacred observances, who did not serve her husband, committed a sin. Kausalya took the admonition with pride, and thereupon conferred benediction on her son.

Rama proceeded to Sita's apartment. Looking on Rama's countenance, and unable to restrain her concern, Sita enquired the reason. Rama replied his father was sending him to the forest in exile and Bharata was to be installed prince regent. "I have come to see you while on my way to the forest. You should live here without extolling my virtues and without offending anyone." Sita said sharply the idea that she should stay behind was unworthy of Rama, who ought to know the duty of a wife! For this very reason, she stood enjoined to accompany him, knowing the hardships in the forest. Rama tried his utmost to dissuade Sita. Sita was resolute, for she could not exist apart from Rama; if she did, she did not live. "Therefore I must accompany you." Rama yielding to her decision, though with grim foreboding, got a foretaste of Sita's gentle firmness of mind.

Hearing the exchange between Rama and Sita, Lakshmana pleaded for permission to go to the forest. Appreciating the deep earnestness, typical of Lakshmana, Rama agreed.

All who witnessed the melancholy scene lamented over the happening. Sage Vasishta, calm of mind yet overwhelmed by sadness, cursed Kaikeyi severely for her cruel act. He hoped Sita would prove a source of solace to Rama in exile.

Thereupon, the king asked Sumantra to bring the chariot to take Rama, Sita and Lakshmana to the forest.

Sita, who had no skill in wearing the bark of trees, erred again and again. She stood embarrassed. Thereupon, Rama going near her personally fastened the bark on her even as Sita had not figured in the king's pledges. Seeing this, women lamented. Vasishta chastised Kaikeyi who had done an unfriendly act to her own son, Bharata! The people wailed loudly. Hearing the cry, Dasaratha roused himself for the last time. He rebuked Kaikeyi for her evil deed. Rama prayed to his father to take care of his noble mother.

Disconsolate and senseless, as it were, Dasaratha wailed his lot. On his orders rare robes and ornaments were put on Sita. Kausalya blessed her. Sita said that she would not deviate from her duty to her husband. Hearing the pledge, Kausalya shed tears of agony as well as of joy. Witnessing this, Rama beseeched his mother not to look on his father with a doleful countenance and promised he would return as his exile ended. The whole palace was filled with wails of agony. Rama, Sita and Lakshmana, with joined palms went round Dasaratha, and bowed to Kausalya, Kaikeyi and Sumitra. Kissing the head of Lakshmana, as he saluted her, Sumitra told him 'excessively fond as you are of Rama, you are accompanying him in his exile'. Gentle by nature and known for her rare reticence, Sumitra tendered Lakshmana her advice which has become a most celebrated quatrain:

ramam dasaratham viddhi mam vidhi janakatmajam
ayodhyamatavim viddhi gachha thatha yathasukham

(Deem Rama as Dasaratha, deem (Sita) daughter of Janaka, as me (your mother), deem the forest as Ayodhya, go happily.)

To Rama she said, "Fare forth! May good happen to you."

Sita, Rama and Lakshmana fell at the feet of Dasaratha before parting. They mounted the chariot, which decked in gold, shone as fire. It had horses moving like wind. Sorely stricken with agony, the people of Ayodhya, young and old, rushed forward to Rama, in the words of the poet, 'in the same way as one oppressed with the sun's heat rushed towards cool water'. Clinging to the sides and rear of the chariot, they prayed to Sumantra to hold its reins. People in thousands ran after the chariot. Rama, unwavering, sensing the situation, commanded the chariot to be driven fast. The chariot sped, carrying the mighty-armed Rama driven out of the city. Dasaratha fell down precipitately like a tree cut at the roots.

The gods, who were witnessing the poignant situation unfolding, rejoiced. "Rama has commenced his mission on the earth!"

Passing beyond the sight of the distressed citizens, the chariot approached the Ganga. The river carrying cool waters was adorned with hermitages on its sides. Rama watched the river in its different moods, as it coursed down, at times turbulent, noisy and full of foam being churned around, at places still and deep, and again agitated, hemmed in by spacious banks, and made noisy by swans and cranes, and decked with flowers and fruit trees.

Reaching near Sringaverapura, the chariot halted under the shade of a large tree laden abundantly with flowers and fresh leaves. The territory was ruled by Guha, a forester by birth, a dear friend of Rama. Hearing of Rama's arrival, Guha waited with his retinue. Welcoming Rama, Guha warmly embraced the prince, and offered him all services, "This principality is as much yours as Ayodhya." Guha had brought cooked rice and a variety of food and drinks, and other offerings. Rama declined these, being under the vow to practise austerities. With sunset, Rama and Sita lay on the ground to repose. Lakshmana and Guha, armed with bow and arrow, kept vigil, with no sleep through the night.

In the morning, on the suggestion of Rama, Guha brought a beautiful boat for the party to cross the Ganga. Thereafter, Rama asked Sumantra to return speedily to Ayodhya.

Rama, Sita and Lakshmana took bath in the river, and rested under the shade of a tree. Clad in the bark of trees and wearing matted locks, Rama and Lakshmana looked charming and radiant like rishis. Deciding to restrict their food to wild fruits, roots and bulbs and to repose on the ground, Rama and Lakshmana observed the vow of an ascetic life. They decided to take their abode in a hermitage in a quiet region.

Rama gave Guha advice on the management of his principality and winning the affection of the people. He bade farewell to Guha.

At the command of Guha, a kinsman of his rowed Rama, Sita and Lakshmana across the river. Sita, with joined palms, addressed the Ganga flowing through heaven, earth and the subterranean regions, a consort of the ocean, as 'goddess' and prayed to protect her lord during his sojourn in the forest.

Reaching its southern bank, Rama told Lakshmana to lead the way, followed by Sita, himself making the rear in protection of both. They soon reached the happy land of Vatsa lying between the Ganga and the Yamuna rivers. It was evening. Resting on the ground covered with straw, grass and leaves, Rama made a last effort to persuade Lakshmana to return to Ayodhya to be with Sumitra. Lakshmana stated he would not enter even a heaven without Rama! Thereupon, Rama vowed to have Lakshmana with him during the period of his exile.

Having spent the night under a big tree, they traversed in the direction of the region where the Yamuna rushed to meet the Ganga. They soon heard the clashing of waters of the two rivers.

Rama, Sita and Lakshmana reached the hermitage of sage Bharadwaja in the vicinity of the confluence of the two rivers. The sage suggested Chitrakoot as the fit place for them to stay. Therefore, they crossed the Yamuna. They halted on its bank. The next morning they moved enjoying the loveliness of the forest, and reached Chitrakoot. They visited the hermitage of sage Valmiki, and decided to stay in the area with his consent. As desired by his brother, Lakshmana erected a hut of leaves for them to stay.

Having heard from Guha of the party leaving for Chitrakoot, Sumantra went back to Ayodhya. Entering the gynaeceum, he reported to Dasaratha and Kausalya the departure of Rama to Chitrakoot. The king and the queen fell into a swoon; Dasaratha waking up swooned again. This happened several times.

While awake, Dasaratha told Kausalya an event that occurred when he was the prince regent. He went out hunting in the forest. It was in the last watch of the night. Hearing a gurgling sound from water nearby, he took it for the trumpeting of an elephant and sent an arrow which hit the target. On approaching the quarry, he discovered to his dismay and sorrow that his shaft had hit a hermit boy, who was collecting water for his aged, blind parents. Dasaratha carried the body to them, and they cursed him that he would also die in agony of separation from his son. After pronouncing the execration, the ascetic couple entered the funeral pyre.

Telling the story, Dasaratha breathed his last. Kausalya, Sumitra and Kaikeyi wailed loudly.

Resting the king's head in her lap, Kausalya severely reproached Kaikeyi: "Having your desire fulfilled, O, cruel one, be satisfied."

Sage Vasishta sent messengers to call back Bharata and Satrughna from the Kekaya kingdom.

The court functionaries reverently consigned the king's body to a trough filled with oil.

On being summoned, Bharata took leave of king Aswapati, his maternal grandfather, and Yudhajit, his uncle, and proceeded to Ayodhya together with Satrughna. Grave apprehensions grew in his mind.

Leaving Rajagriha, crossing rivers, streams, territories, Bharata spent a few nights to reach Ayodhya.

Having reached the palace, he did not find his father in the king's apartments. Bharata went to see his mother, who seeing her son sprang on her feet at once quitting her seat of gold.

In reply to his anxious enquiries, Kaikeyi narrated the events, concluding that his father 'met the same fate as is the destined end of all created beings'.

"Alas, I am ruined!" said Bharata in agony and fell prostrate. His mother said, "O, king, rise, O, illustrious one!" Bharata wept for a long time. Kaikeyi spoke in a tone of giving welcome news about the departure of Rama, Sita and Lakshmana to the Dandaka forest! She said vainly, "Your father was asked by me for the sovereignty of Ayodhya in your favour and the banishment of Rama. Following his truthful nature the king did as I asked him. Stricken with grief, the highly illustrious emperor met his end."

Bitterly reproaching his mother, Bharata vowed to bring back Rama from the forest, and crown him. He was filled with rage.

Kausalya and Bharata, who sought each other, met. She told Bharata: "Enjoy the kingdom secured for you by Kaikeyi through a cruel deed." Bharata said: "Wherefore do you reproach me, O, noble lady? Nay, you know my great love for Rama!" Even while so reassuring, Bharata fell to the ground stricken with agony. Kausalya convinced of his innocence put

47

him on her lap, and wept. Bharata too lamented through grief. The night passed.

On the advice of sage Vasishta, Bharata and Satrughna cremated their father's body with due obsequies, and concluded the rites, as also libations of water on the bank of the Sarayu.

Satrughna blamed Lakshmana for failing to restrain their father in committing the folly. Bharata caught sight of Manthara decked with ornaments. Satrughna sought to punish her but on Bharata's pleading for mercy, he let go the hunchback.

The ceremonies were over on the twelfth day. As Bharata was making preparations to go to the forest, he was urged to be present in the assembly, where Vasishta told the prince: "Sovereignty has been conferred on you by your father and elder brother." Bharata said: "The throne is Rama's. I too belong to Rama!" He vowed to go to Rama and entreat him to accept the crown. The assembly shed tears of joy. "I shall follow Rama alone," he concluded.

Leaving Ayodhya accompanied by Satrughna, family priests, the army and the citizens, Bharata proceeded to the forest in the chariot driven by Sumantra. The queens Kausalya, Kaikeyi and Sumitra travelled in separate chariots. Bharata reached the Ganga at Sringaverapura from where Guha ruled his tribe. Encamping the army, Bharata performed libations of water in honour of his deceased father.

Guha, on gauging Bharata's intentions, entertained the prince and his men with fruits and roots. Acting as a guide, he consoled Bharata, who constantly wailed for Rama.

Bharata set out, along with sage Vasishta, to the hermitage of Bharadwaja. He bowed down at the feet of the sage, and told him of his intention to bring back Rama from the forest. The sage said, "Your brother is at present dwelling on the Chitrakoot hill." The sage, who extended hospitality to the prince, his army

48

and entourage, showed Bharata the way to the hill. Identifying the features on the way, Bharata commanded the army to look for the hermitage of Rama. Seeing smoke at a distance, the army halted and Bharata and Vasishta and a few others walked to the place identified.

While enjoying the scenic delights of Chitrakoot, in the company of Sita, Rama saw a large cloud of dust and heard a loud noise. He despatched Lakshmana to find out the cause. Climbing a tree, Lakshmana saw the army and identified Bharata's distinguished chariot fast approaching the hut. Lakshmana spoke angrily about Bharata who had arrived in state! Rama, who knew the mind of Bharata, pacified his brother.

The army encamped, Bharata himself, with the ministers, walked and hastened in order to meet Rama. Bharata reached the hut; he descried his elder brother, wearing a mass of matted hair, and clad in a strip of bark and the skin of a black buck, seated on ground strewn with kusa (sacred) grass. He saw Sita and Lakshmana by his side. Distressed at the sight, Bharata rushed towards his adorable brother, wailing, "Woe to me, condemned by the world, cruel as I am." He fell down, while attempting to place his hands at the feet of Rama, crying "O, worshipful brother!" His throat was choked. Shedding tears, Satrughna bowed down at the feet of Rama. The latter looked on Bharata fallen on the ground with joined palms, wearing matted locks and clad in bark, pale-faced and emaciated. Rama lifted him, smelt his head in affection, embraced him and placed him in his lap.

Rama tenderly questioned Bharata, "Where I wonder has our father gone (alone), that you have come all the way to the forest? I hope O, gentle brother, your sovereignty, which has come down from eternity, has not been lost, immature as you are."

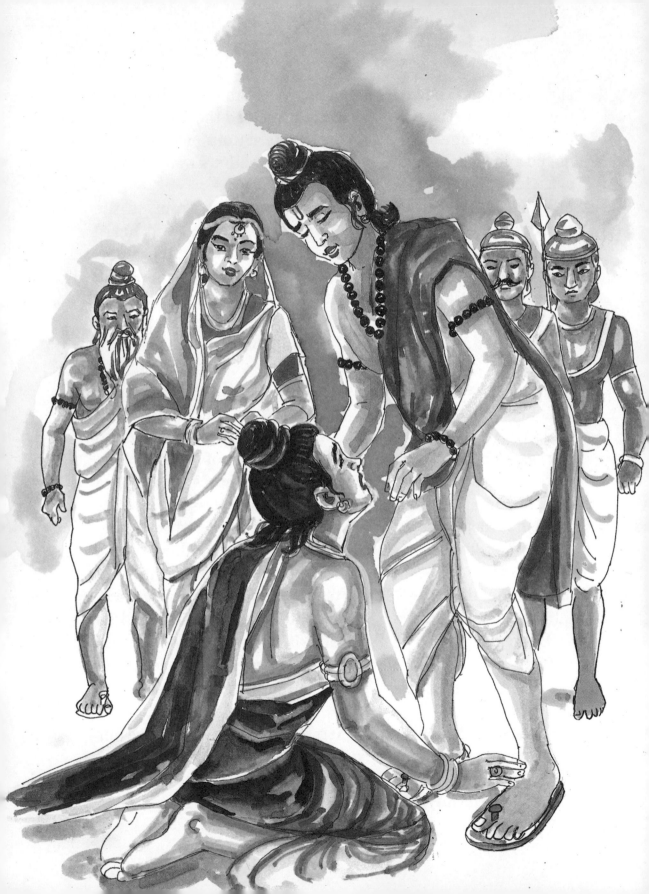

Rama enquired of Vasishta, and Kausalya, Sumitra and Kaikeyi. He enquired earnestly of others.

Rama gave instructions to Bharata on judicature, the art of governance, and his duty of looking after the people.

Rama repeatedly enquired about their father's wellbeing. So questioned, Bharata told Rama, "Bereft of you and stricken with grief caused by separation from you, our father ascended to heaven." Hearing the news, Rama fainted and dropped to the ground 'like a tree with boughs full of blossom felled down with an axe'. Lakshmana wept. Sita, who was blinded by tears, could hardly look on her lord! Regaining consciousness, Rama wailed piteously. All shed copious tears. They duly proceeded to the bank of the Mandakini river and offered water to the spirit of their high-souled father. Coming back to the hut, they completed the performance of the appropriate rites.

The queens accompanied by sage Vasishta went to Rama's hermitage. Rama, Sita and Lakshmana clasped their feet. Kausalya felt sad about Sita's travails in the forest.

Bharata, in deep agony, implored Rama to accept the throne of Ayodhya, which was his. Rama pacified his brother and urged him to assume the rulership of the kingdom on the behest of their father. Thereafter Rama fell silent.

All the arguments of Bharata failed to change Rama's mind.

"I implore you with my head bent low. If you set aside my request and decide to go into the Dandaka forest, I too shall depart with you." The priests and the citizens joined Bharata's plea. Rama, with characteristic stoicism, declined to accept the vicarious task. He addressed Bharata, "For my sake, O, Bharata, exonerate our father from the debt (he owed to Kaikeyi)." Rama stressed its merit, quoting the holy texts: 'One who delivered his father from the hell named 'Put', is called putra (son).' Rama asked Bharata to return, accompanied by Satrughna, their mothers, the priests, the Brahmanas, the army and the citizens, to Ayodhya to protect the people. He would, in the company of Sita and Lakshmana, enter the Dandaka forest without delay. "Let us, his four dutiful sons, enable our father to adhere to truth."

Jabali, an eminent sage, attempted to advise Rama by resorting to the theory of the nastikas (non-believers). "O, Rama, one goes back to the elements from which he has sprung. Such is the way of created things whereas you are harassed for no purpose." Rama, who knew ever what was right, denounced the materialistic concept rooted in the world of senses, and rebuked Jabali. The latter begged forgiveness for making a heretic speech in order to pacify the prince.

Even on Vasishta's suggestion to grant the prayer of Bharata, Rama refused. His mothers' pleas, added to Bharata's prayer failed. He ruled out Bharata's proposal to fast unto death, or remain in the forest.

Bharata's entreaty to Rama to assume rulership, and Rama's refusal repeated several times.

Heavenly beings, who heard the dialogue between Rama and Bharata applauded Rama's conduct. The rishis, who longed for the destruction of Ravana, exhorted Bharata, "The advice of Rama ought to be accepted by you."

Bharata prayed to Rama for mercy. He placed a pair of sandals decked with gold in front of Rama, requesting him to place his feet on them. Bharata would rule the kingdom on behalf of Rama, symbolically worshipping the sandals. He insisted Rama should return promptly after the expiry of his exile.

Rama stood on the sandals which Bharata had brought, and leaving them immediately he handed over the sandals to Bharata. The latter accepted them as the symbols of rulership on behalf of his brother.

Rama confirmed his vow. He looked bright, his face beaming in joy. With palms joined in reverence, Bharata, falling at Rama's feet made a fervent appeal in most endearing terms. "O, Rama, you ought to fulfil the obligation and grant my prayer as well as the wish of Kausalya. I for my part cannot protect the vast dominion single-handed." Rama placed Bharata on his lap, and in sweet persuasiveness replied, "You can very well protect even the earth through the wisdom born of humility that has dawned on you," he said emphatically. "Splendour would sooner depart from the moon, nay, the Himalaya mountain would sooner shed its snow and the ocean would sooner cross its limits than I shall violate the plighted word of my father. Your mother Kaikeyi's conduct should not be taken to heart by you," Rama declared finally.

Worshipfully bowing down to the sandals, Bharata said, "Indeed being delegated the burden of rulership to these sandals, O, gallant brother, I would live solely on fruits and roots for fourteen years, wearing matted locks and the bark of trees, longing for your return and dwelling outside the city."

"So be it," averred Rama. Embracing Bharata and Satrughna, he said, "Take care of mother Kaikeyi, be not angry with her. You are adjured so by me as well as by Sita." His eyes filled with tears, Rama bade goodbye to Bharata. Carrying the sandals, Bharata circumambulated Rama. Paying respect to all those gathered there, preceptors, counsellors, citizens, Bharata and Satrughna, Rama steadfast in duty sent them back. Saluting his mothers, Rama entered the cottage.

On the way to Ayodhya, Bharata paid his respect to sage Bharadwaja, and crossed the Yamuna and Ganga rivers. Departing from Sringaverapura he caught sight of Ayodhya.

When the queens had entered its gynaeceum, with the blessing of sage Vasishta, Bharata proceeded to Nandigrama on the city's periphery. He installed the sandals on the royal seat. He put on the garb of an ascetic and commenced to rule the kingdom at the behest of his brother's sandals holding the royal umbrella over them.

Bharata having departed, Rama noticed the ascetics living in the area perturbed, and anxious to leave it. He sought the reason. The ascetics answered they were scared of a mighty demon, Khara, and a large number of ogres in the nearby Janasthana, who plagued them, assuming savage, hideous and ugly forms.

Not desiring to prolong the stay in Chitrakoot, Rama, Sita and Lakshmana left the place. They reached the hermitage of Atri who extended hospitality to them. His aged wife, Anasuya, who was distinguished by severe austerities and practice of virtue, welcomed Sita. The latter told of her marriage to Rama, his self-abnegation honouring the pledge of his father, and their coming to the forest. Highly pleased, Anasuya bestowed on Sita a celestial garland, a garment and ornaments. The princes and Sita stayed with the ascetics during night. In the morning the party left the ashrama following the route shown by the hermits to the Dandaka forest.

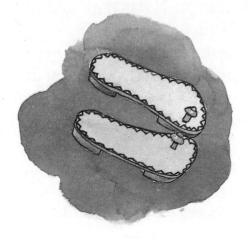

ARANYA KANDA

Abduction

Rama, Sita and Lakshmana entered the dense forest, Dandaka. The word meant affliction.

In it stood several hermitages, from which emanated the chanting of prayers and religious hymns. Their floors were littered with kusa grass, faggots made of barks, sacrificial utensils, fruits and flowers. A haunt of birds, sporting deer and other gentle creatures, the abodes of the ascetics were visited by celestials who sang and danced. The ashramas shrouded in nature and resounding with the cadences of prayers and sacred sounds merged with the peaceful environment.

Seeing the holy abodes, Rama unwound his bow. As the party entered these, the ascetics, their disciples and other dwellers were struck by the beauty and benevolent demeanour and grandeur of Rama. They were filled with pure joy. They looked at Sita and Lakshmana with love and wonder.

The ascetics welcomed the princes and the princess with roots, fruits and flowers. They offered the guests their own hermitages and sought Rama's protection. Having received the hospitality, the party took leave of the sages. By sunrise they went deep into the forest. It was dark and dreadful, with wild animals roaming about.

Rama, Sita and Lakshmana saw an ogre, massive as a mountain peak, with a huge open mouth, from which dangled dead deer, wolves, tigers, lions, and the head of an elephant! Holding a mighty lance, he roared with a terrible voice, "I wander eating the flesh of sages." This was Viradha. Sita trembled.

Viradha seized and carried Sita in his arms. He gloated he had attained, through penance, invulnerability to any weapon. Thereupon Rama stringed his bow and discharged seven arrows

56

with golden feathers. These pierced the giant. Dropping Sita, he fell drenched in blood. Rising, Viradha rushed towards the princes with his flaming mouth. They shot a volley of arrows. Viradha caught the princes in his arms and strode far into the forest, which reverberated with his furious roar. Sita cried aloud. The royal pair broke the demon's arms.

Mangled, Viradha revealed he was a gandharva, named Tumburu, under a curse, who was waiting for Rama to liberate him. He advised Rama to meet on his way a sage, Sarabhanga. On his request, the brothers threw the ogre's body into a pit. Leaving the earthly body, the gandharva soared into the sky. Rama, Sita and Lakshmana moved on happily.

Sage Sarabhanga advised Rama to seek the blessings of an austere ascetic, Sutikshna who dwelt in a charming region, upstream of the river Mandakini. After blessing Rama, Sarabhanga gave up his body by entering fire.

Sutikshna offered the guests his own abode abounding in roots, fruits and flowers, and frequented by beautiful deer. After passing the night there, on the advice of the sage, Rama, Sita and Lakshmana went into the forest. It shone with flowers, lakes and ponds with crystalline waters and receiving springs flowing down the hills and lively with herds of deer and flocks of birds.

As they walked on, Sita was given to grave misgivings and was perturbed. She ventured to forewarn her husband. For, Rama, who was armed, might cause injury to the forest-dwellers and its creatures. His killing the ogres, without a cause, could be a folly. The prince, valorous by nature, could subtly be led away from dharma. Sita had her logic. Rama, bound by his pledge, was to live as an ascetic during his exile; therefore, his actions in the forest as a Kshatriya prone to heroic deeds would not be compatible. Killing for sport was not right. He should devote himself solely and strictly to righteousness.

She explained gently. A pious ascetic lived in a holy forest, where animals abounded and moved freely in joy. Lord Indra, who wanted to break the saint's austerities, came in disguise to the hermitage, and left a sword in its precincts. It was a calculated act. The weapon came handy to the ascetic, who carried it even when he set out to fetch roots and fruits for his food. He became inhibited by an urge to use the weapon always. The habit warped his mind. Slowly giving up his austerities, he used the sword for wrong purposes! The possession of the sword totally changed him. A weapon in hand tempted its owner to use it even unjustly and wantonly. "O, lord, your present status, though being a Kshatriya, is that of an ascetic, it is not related to killing." Sita begged forgiveness for her frivolity in daring to talk thus to Rama who possessed all the wisdom in the three worlds.

Rama was touched by the logic of Sita's words. He, however, recalled his commitment to the sages to protect them from the ogres who harassed them. He would not easily falsify his plighted word to his father. Sita's advice, which showed foresight, pleased Rama.

As the group went deeper, they saw many mountain peaks and beautiful rivers. The animal life in the forest was fascinating—cranes on riverbanks, aquatic birds, varieties of deer, horned buffaloes in rut, boars and elephants. In the golden rays of the setting sun, they saw a lake adorned with red and white lotuses, with elephant herds and crowded with cranes and swans. They heard sounds of singing, and of musical instruments played by unseen nymphs, who bathed in the lake.

The party visited many beauty spots, holy places and hermitages. Years passed.

After the wanderings, they came back to Sutikshna's abode, as had been advised.

The sage guided Rama to go in the southerly direction and to meet sage Agasthya of blazing lustre, and celebrated for his extraordinary powers and deeds.

On their way they saw many forests, the trees bending down with loads of fruits and masses of flowers. The scent of the ripe pippali (pepper) came wafted in wind.

The sage's hermitage stood in a delightful part of the forest. Rama told Lakshmana and Sita about Agasthya. He was a sage among sages. He protected the forests and made them inhabitable. The Vindhya mountain, obeying his command, did not obstruct the path of the sun. "Here I shall adore the great sage and stay in the region for the rest of our exile," Rama said.

Agasthya himself, at the head of seers, came forward to receive Rama, and welcomed the royal party.

Sage Agasthya gave Rama, among other mystic missiles, the bow of God Vishnu, and two inexhaustible quivers of arrows, and a sword. These were foremost weapons. He praised Sita, who in her constancy, was like Arundhati, consort of Vasishta.

The sage advised Rama to proceed to a place close to the nearby Godavari river, abounding in roots, flowers and fruits, and lively with diverse flocks of birds and deer. This was Panchavati. It was charming. Sita would rejoice there.

Taking leave of the sage, the party on their way met a gigantic vulture. The latter declared himself to be a friend of king Dasaratha. He was Jatayu, son of Aruna, who was brother of Garuda, the mount of God Vishnu. His elder brother was Sampathi. Jatayu pledged to guard Sita.

The party reached Panchavati, with its woodlands in blossom. Rama chose a spot for a hermitage. While they stayed there happily, the winter season set in. The poet gave, in the words of Lakshmana, a sensitive description of winter enveloping the forest.

In the ritu (season), that was welcome to all, nature looked blessed. As the sun veered to the south, the northern region was no more charming than a lady without tilak (auspicious mark on forehead); the sun decked in snow being away, the Himalaya justified its name (abode of snow). Free from the tyranny of heat, the day remained calm. The night was reposeful. The moon looked pale, like a mirror soiled with exhalation. The westerly winds blew cold towards dawn.

Shrouded in mist and rich with crops of paddy, barley and wheat, the woodlands appeared attractive. The sun, wrapped in fog, though risen high, resembled the moon! The grass was lightly drenched with dew drops. The elephants, though seized with thirst, withdrew their trunks from the cold waters. The birds did not fight. The lotuses worn out and blasted by snow were reduced to mere stalks.

Lakshmana concluded by saying that in that season, Bharata, who returned from Chitrakoot, practised austerities out of devotion to Rama. Abjuring luxuries, he reposed on the bare earth. He remained truthful, polite and amiable, and emulated Rama in asceticism. The people saw how deeply he was benign unlike his mother Kaikeyi! Rama cautioned Lakshmana that Kaikeyi should never be condemned. He longed for reunion with the high-souled Bharata and the heroic Satrughna.

Seated with Sita and Lakshmana in the hut thatched with leaves, Rama shone brightly like the moon. Lakshmana gained wisdom as his brother discussed various subjects with him.

At this time, ogress Surpanakha reached the place, called Janasthana. Seeing Rama, with his radiant countenance, lotus eyes, majestic gait, yet exuding tenderness, she got infatuated with vile longing. She introduced herself to the princes. She was sister of Ravana, lord of Lanka, and of Kumbhakarna of immense size and prowess, and of Vibhishana who was pious-minded. They dwelt in Lanka. Her other brothers were Khara and Dushana, who were fierce in their valour and had huge armies. Endowed with superhuman powers, Surpanakha could range at will, assuming any form she chose. She would be a becoming wife for Rama!

Rama rejected her overture. Surpanakha approached Lakshmana. He too rejected her.

Infuriated, the demoness rushed upon Sita.

Lakshmana intervened. He lopped off Surpanakha's ears and nose. The fierce ogress, mangled and drenched in blood,

62

ran into the forest with uproarious thundering.

Surpanakha hurried to Khara. Falling on the ground, she narrated her encounter with Rama, Sita and Lakshmana.

The humiliation of his sister filled Khara with sorrow and anger. He commanded a few powerful ogres to go to Janasthana to avenge his sister's discomfiture. They sped like clouds.

Struck by Rama's arrows, the ogres fell. Hearing of the event, Khara, who was reproached by Surpanakha, sallied forth, with Dushana and Trisira, his generals, commanding an army of fourteen thousand dreadful demons. They were equipped with

formidable weapons. Khara sped furiously in his chariot filling the air with its sound.

The rishis longed to witness the encounter between Khara and Rama. The celestials, who filled the sky, prayed for Rama's victory. The vast rakshasa army moved towards Rama and Lakshmana like innumerable planets rushing on the sun and the moon. Rama noticed the omens foreboding vast destruction. Rama's arms quivered in joy and his mighty bow bestirred. Lakshmana looked radiant. The poet said Rama was forbidding in form, for action.

The demons struck Rama with clubs, barbed missiles, swords and axes. Rama, though besmeared with blood, pulled thousands of arrows and sent them against the hordes. Fleeing in the air, after cleaving the bodies of the ogres, his arrows reddened with blood looked like flashes of fire. His bow, bent to a circle, rained arrows, which destroyed the demons, their weapons, coats of mail, horses, and charioteers and all. The army was thrown into disarray.

The rakshasas attacked Rama from all sides. The stream of arrows from Rama's bow, so fast to be visible, hid the sky, and rained destruction.

The fourteen thousand ogres had fallen dead! Dushana fell. Trisira, with his three heads, confronted Rama. Facing a volley of arrows, Rama, who was enraged, struck down the enemy's swift-footed horses and the charioteer, and pierced the ogre in his heart as he fell from his chariot. Rama struck off the heads of the ogre.

Rallying the remaining ogres, Khara rushed forward.

Came the battle between Khara and Rama. Bewildered by the destruction of his immense army by Rama single-handed, Khara attacked. Riding in his chariot, Khara sent mystic missiles and filled all quarters with arrows. Bending his mighty bow, Rama covered the entire sky with arrows that resembled flashes of fire. The sun became invisible. Splitting Rama's bow, Khara tormented him, and made his bright armour to fall. Rama now wielded God Vishnu's bow, which sage Agasthya gave him. He cut down Khara's gold ensign, the yoke of his chariot, its horses, and the charioteer. He shattered the enemy's bow. Jumping down from the chariot, Khara brandished a mace in his hand.

Rama addressed Khara: "One, who was hard-hearted and oppressive, would not survive, be he the ruler of the three worlds. You killed the ascetics in the Dandaka forest wantonly. I shall destroy you today."

Khara retorted, "Having destroyed my army, you brag. I shall avenge their death." The blazing mace, resembling a thunderbolt released by Khara, which reduced the trees and shrubs to ashes, drew close to Rama. The prince shattered it in the air.

Deprived of weapon, Khara uprooted a sal tree and, whirling it, hurled it on Rama, saying 'you are killed'. Rama, with his eyes reddened in anger, cut down the tree, and pierced Khara with a thousand arrows. With blood gushing forth from his wounds, and maddened, Khara rushed on Rama who, stepping back deftly, discharged the arrow gifted by Lord Indra. It hit Khara in the chest with a thunderlike clap. Burnt by the flaming shaft, Khara fell to the ground.

The celestials rained flowers and praised Rama for his wonderful feat—destruction of fourteen thousand ogres, of Dushana, Trisira and Khara himself in a brief part of a day! The rishis including sage Agasthya marvelled at Rama's heroism.

Rama returned to his hermitage. Sita's countenance glowed with admiration.

The news of the extinction of the vast horde and the killing of Dushana, Trisira and Khara by Rama reached Ravana through

Akampana, a rakshasa who hastened from Janasthana. Boundless indignation turned his twenty eyes bloodshot. He heard about Rama's extraordinary prowess and glory. Rama's brother, Lakshmana, was like him in valour! Rama's spouse, Sita was the noblest of women endowed with rare beauty!

Hearing the incredible account, two passions began obsessing Ravana's mind. One was vengeance, the other was Sita! Yet, having heard of Rama's heroism, he preferred discretion to be the better part of valour. He should achieve his end through guile.

Travelling in his aerial chariot, Ravana reached Maricha, his uncle, in his hermitage. The latter heard the deed of Rama at Janasthana. Ravana, who planned to abduct Sita, said, "Lend me your help."

Remembering his own encounter with Rama at sage Viswamitra's sacrifice, Maricha said, "You are ill-advised to abduct Sita, which will lead to fighting Rama of infinite glory. Leave Sita alone." So warned, Ravana returned to Lanka.

Meanwhile, Surpanakha, who was thwarted by the princes, reached Ravana and reported her humiliation and disfiguration. She twitted him, "A frightful danger awaits you. Your spies have failed. Your laziness is unbecoming a great king." She added shrewdly: "Sita, with the lustre of molten gold and with her beauty of form, shone like Lakshmi! Indeed she merits being your consort."

Ravana was thrilled. He made up his mind.

Infatuated by the thought of Sita, he sped in his golden car to Maricha. He would avenge his sister's discomfiture by abducting Sita. He said, "Apart from possessing strength, you are adept in conjuring tricks. You should use these. You should take the form of a golden deer and lure Rama and Lakshmana away from Sita for a while. I shall take her away."

The plan alarmed Maricha. He warned: "I do not attempt to please you by speaking agreeable words. I am not one such. Your plan to deceive Rama could be death itself for you, and your entire race. Sita would be the cause." He once more recalled his plight at sage Viswamitra's sacrifice. He escaped, because Rama never hit a fugitive! The event forced him to turn a recluse and he took to austerities and to practice of yoga. He saw Rama everywhere, even in his dreams. Therefore, if Ravana entered into hostilities with Rama, a terrible fate awaited him. The fabulous Lanka would be laid waste on account of Sita. The rarer virtue lay in forbearance.

Ravana did not accept his uncle's advice. "A monarch should be obeyed; defiance would recoil with instant death."

Maricha replied devoid of fear, "Take me as killed at the very sight of Rama and deem yourself as dead as soon as you bear away Sita." The poet observed 'men who worked their own ruin did not listen to salutary advice tendered by the discerning. 'Vinasa kale vipareeta buddhi' (destined to doom, perversity grips its victim).

Ravana and Maricha flew to Rama's hermitage.

Reaching there, Maricha, using the art of illusion, turned into a deer of rare beauty. It paced at the entrance of the hut.

The poet's portrait of the animal was an example of word power! 'It was a deer alluring with the tips of its horns bright as sapphire, its head a blend of white and dark, its snout mingling the hues of the white and blue lotuses, its ears shining, likewise its belly, its flanks pale as the softest flower. Its tail had the beauty of the rainbow. Its delicate legs had hoofs glowing like a cat's-eye gem. Its simmering form, like minerals, was soul-captivating. Its slender, foamy mouth illumined the forest. With hundreds of golden and silvery spots, the rare creature was a picture of enchantment.'

The animal moved in front of the hermitage, nibbling tender shoots. It vanished and appeared amidst herds of deer. Coming close to Sita, the stag spun around like a golden stream.

Plucking flowers, Sita sighted the antelope with pearl-like spots. Filled with wonder and sheer joy, she called out for Rama and Lakshmana.

The princes, who arrived, saw the strange creature. Lakshmana suspected deception, for no deer so embellished existed on the earth. It was a phantom, he said. Interrupting him, Sita told Rama the deer fascinated her mind and heart. "I long for the lovely one. Fetch it." Sita added her desire may be thought unworthy of her. "My mind has been captivated by its weird beauty." Rama's mind was filled with curiosity by the golden deer, its flamelike tongue shedding lustre around.

Rama told Lakshmana it looked a wondrous animal; if it was a phantom, it must be put an end to or "I shall capture it." He

enjoined on Lakshmana to guard Sita at any cost, and not to move from the place and to exercise utmost vigilance. He said that Jatayu, the mighty bird, a good friend of theirs, was nearby.

Lakshmana's suspicions deepened.

Rama pursued the deer. Out of dread, Maricha vanished for a while. The creature again came in view. As Rama drew near, every time the deer ran out of sight, and reappeared. Leaping in, darting away, the animal looked like the 'orb of the autumnal moon amidst the fragmented clouds.' Thus tantalizing, the rakshasa drew Rama far away from the hermitage.

Rama, who felt puzzled, paused as the deer issued from a cluster of trees. He remembered the grave doubts voiced by Lakshmana. Training a blazing arrow to his bow, he sent it in full fury. Coursing like lightning, it pierced the heart of the deer. It fell. Falling, it assumed the true gigantic form of Maricha and, as had been advised by Ravana, emulated

Rama's voice to wail! "Alas, Sita! Ah, Lakshmana!"

Lakshmana's misgivings having come true, Rama's mind instantly turned to Sita. Filled with apprehension, he wondered if Sita heard the demon's false cry!

Hearing the cry, as if from her lord, Sita said: "Rama is in dire distress. Rush at once to your brother, possibly fallen into the hands of the demons."

Lakshmana did not stir from where he stood.

Seeing this, Sita spoke in unusual ire, "Son of Sumitra, you act as if you were an enemy in the guise of a brother and you wish Rama to perish! You ought to be with Rama in this predicament. You stand unperturbed; is it for reason of your greed for me?"

Lakshmana in deepest anguish rejoined: "Your lord is unconquerable even by the gods. It was not his voice we heard; it was a conjuring trick. You are a sacred trust in my charge. I dare not leave you alone. O, blessed lady, shed your agony."

Riven by rage outrunning her noble serenity, her eyes turning blood-red with anger, Sita uttered the harshest words: "You are ignoble, a blot on your race! Rama's plight is your opportunity! You were possibly engaged by Bharata. Your greed shall not be satisfied, or Bharata's purpose achieved. I am to end my life instantly, and in your presence."

Stung to his soul, Lakshmana was in indescribable sorrow. He, who had mastered his senses, submitted with joined palms: "You are a deity to me, these words are not worthy of the princess of Videha, these fell from your lips." He added by way of a testament: "Such has been the nature of woman, fickle, hard-hearted, and a cause for discord. Let the denizens of the forest be my solemn witnesses. You face danger! I leave. Let the sylvan deities protect you." Bathed in hot gushing tears, Lakshmana, in deep reverence yet tried to disabuse the mind of Sita in agony and concern. Sita remained impassive! Bowing down, Soumitri departed, looking back at her with every few steps.

Sita was left alone.

Seeing the opportunity, Ravana transformed himself into a wandering recluse, clad in ochre-coloured garments with a tuft of hair on his head, carrying an umbrella on his right shoulder, and bearing a staff and a kamandalu (vessel made of coconut shell) on his left shoulder. He advanced fast to Sita.

The poet said perceiving the tragic situation, the trees in Janasthana dared not to wave, nor the wind to blow. The Godavari river slowed in its course.

With his eyes fixed intently on the princess, the mendicant stood before the distressed Sita. He gazed at her rare form and beauty made more pronounced by grief. Ravana, who had masterly skill in articulation, extolled her excellence in chosen words: "O, rare lady, with dark eyes, and a sweet smile, this forest is the abode of ogres and wild animals! It is full of danger. Who are you?"

Superbly praised, Sita, though in agony, did her duty by attempting to honour the ascetic; she offered him a seat, and food, with courtesy. Sita cast her eyes around for Rama and Lakshmana. Answering Ravana's question, Sita told about Rama's disrupted coronation (vichchinnabhisheka), his acceptance of exile to uphold his father's pledge, and her accompanying Rama to the forest. She asked the visitor to identify his name and descent.

The anchorite replied, "I am Ravana, ruler of the rakshasas, reigning from Lanka, girt by the southern ocean. Become the foremost queen among my many consorts."

Enraged, Sita said, "I am devoted to the mighty-armed Rama. You covet me! You who seek me through deceit will, without doubt, meet your doom."

Ravana boasted of his descent, strength and feats of war to intimidate her. Sita was not daunted. Brimming with anger, she warned that one who treated her with indignity would not survive. Such was the power of Rama.

Rebuked, Ravana manifested his enormous form. His ten heads wore lustrous diadem(s) and his twenty arms shone with rare ornaments. "I can toss the earth on my arms, I can annihilate death itself. I can take any form at will." His twenty eyes burned like fire. "You deserve a husband known in the three worlds, betake yourself to me. Rama is hardly an equal to me."

Even as the consciousness of his past misdeeds and their possible nemesis lay in his mind, Ravana overcome with desire, hoisted Sita and placed her in his chariot. Acutely agonized, Sita called out, "O, Rama." She struggled in vain. The car rose into the air. Sita wailed loudly, calling out the names of Lakshmana and Rama again and again.

Sita being borne away caught the sight of Jatayu who was perched on a tree. She called out to him. "Look at me being carried away by this cruel predator. He is incapable of being stopped. I pray, report my abduction to Rama."

Jatayu, who was lying fast asleep, heard the call. He saw Ravana in his chariot. Huge in size, with a sharp bill, he challenged the king of Lanka. A tumultuous encounter followed. Even as assailed by sharp arrows, the mighty vulture, with wild talons, wounded Ravana's body and limbs. He broke his weapons one after another, cut his coat of mail, killed the mules, smashed the chariot, and struck off the head of the charioteer. Ravana fell to the ground.

All beings hailed Jatayu's deeds. Ravana, carrying Sita, rose in the sky. Jatayu flew to Ravana and intercepted him, saying: "You are a coward, not a hero. Fight me," swooping all over

with his claws, wings and bill. Ravana so tormented was terrified, and seethed with rage. Nearly being overwhelmed in the duel that followed, Ravana unsheathed his invincible celestial sword and with it slashed Jatayu's wings, feet and flanks instantly. The fabulous bird fell to the ground, lying like 'an extinguished forest fire'.

Sita, free from Ravana's grip, embraced the bird who fought for the cause of Rama. Ravana seized Sita by her hair. Watching the harrowing act, the forest, its animals and birds stood enveloped in darkness. The sun lost its lustre, the wind stood still. The rishis in the forest felt agonized even as they looked for the destruction of Ravana.

God Brahma, seeing Ravana inviting his own disaster, exclaimed: "Our purpose is being accomplished!"

Ravana fled through the air carrying Sita, who in captivity shone like 'lightning amidst a dark cloud'.

Seeing Sita's plight, lotuses which had lent their beauty to her features fainted; lions, tigers and other beasts and birds rushed following her flying shadow. The forest deities panicked, the alarmed fawns wore dejected looks, and all beings lamented.

Being borne over, Sita rebuked Ravana. "All the worlds will reproach you. You are caught in the noose of death."

Sita, left to her own wits, looked down on the earth. She saw a few big vanaras (monkeys) on a mountain top. She took off a few of her ornaments and, wrapping them in a part of her silken garment, dropped them hoping the monkeys would see the jewels and give Rama a possible clue to the direction of Ravana's flight. The latter did not notice Sita's action. The monkeys who looked up heard the lady crying loudly.

In the conceit of his misdeed, Ravana coursed fast over forests, rivers, mountains and lakes. Spanning the southern ocean, he reached Lanka.

Ravana lodged Sita in his own gynaeceum. He left her in the care of frightful ogresses, who were warned against uttering harsh words to Sita. He commanded powerful demons to bring news about Rama.

The poet said Ravana remained happy through unwisdom.

The lord of Lanka was moved by passion, which made him act foolishly. He saw Sita given over to woe, amidst ogresses. She sat with her head bent down shedding tears.

Ravana talked to his captive, even as she was most disinclined to listen to him. He described the glory of his palace! It stood on pillars of ivory, gold, crystal and silver, studded with diamonds. The stairways were made of gold. These were embellished with refined gold. Above the stairways were rows of palaces, with floors inlaid with gems. The wells and ponds within were gorgeous with flowers of various kinds. He vowed that all the palaces, mansions, treasures, and his kingdom were Sita's, pleading she may look on him favourably. He concluded 'Do not hope to see Rama again.'

Letting her tears to flow, and covering her face, Sita spoke, warning: "By creating enmity to Rama, you have embraced death, your folly will cause Lanka to be widowed."

Enraged, Ravana threatened; he gave Sita twelve months to change her mind. If she did not, she would become a morsel for him. He ordered that Sita be placed in the beautiful asoka grove, guarded by rakshasa women. The latter would employ threats and conciliation alternately to win over Sita.

Sad beyond words, Sita thought of Rama and Lakshmana.

Lord Indra came to Sita and, remaining invisible to others, gave her celestial food and drink to keep hunger and thirst away from her. The gods were pleased that the scheme of Rama destroying Ravana was progressing.

In the Dandaka forest, Rama, after killing Maricha, hastened to the hermitage. He was filled with deep anxiety. If Sita had heard Maricha's words simulating his voice, would Lakshmana be persuaded to leave her? This thought had oppressed his mind. As he walked, bad portents occurred. The beasts and birds, which passed him, cried fearfully. The nature around drooped.

Was all well with Sita?

Halfway Rama met Lakshmana. His brother looked crestfallen and sorely afflicted. Did he come, abandoning Sita in the lonely forest? If so, Lakshmana did a reproachful act, inasmuch as Sita needed protection. His mind was agitated. Seeing Lakshmana in utter anguish and perplexed as never before, Rama asked his brother to say what happened. Yet reposed in mind he put the question many times. "Where is Sita, who followed me to the Dandaka forest, who is dearer to me than my own life?" No words from Lakshmana came forth.

Entering the ashrama Rama did not find Sita!

As Rama enquired without respite, Lakshmana, whose intense sorrow dried up his tears, unfolded what had happened. When he insisted on the voice of the demon as being a hoax, the words uttered by Sita were unbearably cruel! Rama was aghast. He said tersely that his brother had done an unbecoming act, letting himself be goaded by the words uttered by an angry woman, and falling a prey to folly! Rama's behest was not done.

The premises of the hermitage bore a melancholy look. The trees stood still as if in pain.

Rama wailed. He wailed again and again, walking on the slopes of mountains, on the banks of rivers. He hurried from tree to tree enquiring, "Where is Sita? Where is Sita?" The forest echoed his agonized lament. He queried the deer if they had seen Sita, whose eyes resembled theirs. Rama and Lakshmana ranged over peaks, caves, cascades, rivers, valleys, chasms,

lakes, along the Godavari river in search of Sita. A herd of large
deer moved in their tract. "Where is Sita?" asked Rama. Thus
addressed, the herd sprang on their feet all of a sudden, and
turned their heads towards the south.

Taking this as a gesture, the brothers travelled in the
southerly direction. They saw a track on the earth with flowers
scattered on the ground, imprints of the feet of a lady in a chaotic
fashion, as also imprints of the feet of an ogre! They examined
the spot. They saw broken arms, a quiver and wrecked chariot
parts. They saw particles of gold, fallen ornaments. The scene
appeared to have been the ground of a big conflict. There lay a
large bow encrusted with pearls and gems, and an armour of
gold embellished with cat's-eye gems lying shattered. They saw

a canopy adorned with celestial wreaths lay dashed to the ground. There lay a chariot of war, with a broken ensign, and a slain charioteer with the lash and reins in his hand.

Was Sita killed? The sight brought intense agony to Rama. Lakshmana tried to becalm his brother.

As the brothers stood caught in a puzzle, they came across Jatayu, fallen on the ground and his huge form drenched in blood. Shaking with death pangs, the vulture spoke in piteous accents: "The godly Sita was taken away by Ravana. I flew to her succour, fighting the demon. I broke his bow, his arrows and smashed his chariot and the charioteer, all lying here in wreckage around. I got my wings severed by his sword. Ravana flew away with Sita towards the south."

Rama embraced Jatayu, who yielded up his life. Mourning the tragic end of one, who was a friend of their father, Rama and Lakshmana cremated Jatayu with full ceremonies.

Going beyond Janasthana, the brothers penetrated into the Krauncha forest. As they proceeded, they saw the hermitage of sage Matanga midway in a dreadful forest. They came across a demoness of gigantic size, Ayomukhi. She seized Lakshmana, who assailed her. She ran away in fright.

A loud noise rended the forest. Seeking to find out the cause, the brothers saw a demon of massive size with a vest, firm and broad chest, a colossal trunk, but no neck or head, with his mouth in the belly, and with one fiery eye! This was Kabandha. Baring his big teeth, and extending his long arms, he blocked the way. He seized the princes together.

The brothers severed Kabandha's arms. He fell, thundering. He asked who the brothers were. Lakshmana told the story of their exile in the forest and the loss of Sita.

Kabandha told his own story. Endowed with extraordinary might, he harassed all beings, including rishis. He was cursed to be an ugly giant. He would regain his original form and glory when his arms got lopped off by Rama.

The brothers cremated Kabandha in the hollow of a mountain. His spirit rose high from the funeral pyre. Regaining his supersensuous memory, Kabandha, seated in a splendid aerial car, foretold the success of Rama in finding Sita. To achieve this purpose, Rama should seek the help of the monkey chief, Sugriva who, dispossessed of his kingdom by his brother Bali, was in distress and lived, along with his ministers, on top of the Rishyamuka hill. Son of sun god, he possessed extraordinary prowess, energy and resolution, and would remain true to his promise. He was in dread of king Bali, who had no match in might. Rama should accept Sugriva's friendship.

Kabandha indicated to the brothers the path through the woodlands. Trees of many kinds abounded, bearing fruits and flowers, dripping honey during all the seasons which occurred simultaneously.

The forest was thick with trees of various kinds, such as jambu (rose apple), jackfruit, banyan, peepul, mango, kadamba, asoka, red sandalwood, and many others. As they went along, they passed through another woodland. This had trees bearing fruits during all the seasons. Lovely swans, ducks and other birds swam on the waters in the ponds and lakes.

Significantly the poet added, 'Having not known destruction before, they were not frightened to see human beings.'

Sages lived there, who were pupils of sage Matanga after whom the forest was called Matangavana. Sabari, their female attendant, lived there.

After advising Rama and Lakshmana, Kabandha shining brightly in the air departed.

At the hermitage on the bank of the Pampa, the princes met Sabari. She bathed their feet, and offered them fruits of every

81

description. After honouring Rama the lady, who wore matted hair and was clad in bark of trees, cast herself into fire. Her soul rose to heaven illumining the forest.

The princes proceeded to the Rishyamuka hill. Seeing the turn of events, Rama's mind gladdened.

They reached the Pampa sarovar (lake). It was most delightful. With its crystal-like water covered with rosy lotuses, clusters of white water lilies and other flowers, it looked like a carpet in many colours. On its bank stood the hill on which Sugriva had taken refuge.

The rapturous description of the woodlands and the Pampa sarovar showed how much the poet had watched nature and how much his poetry imbibed it.

KISHKINDHA KANDA

An Ally

Rama and Lakshmana approached the Rishyamuka hill. Watching them, the monkey chief, Sugriva took them to be possibly agents of his brother, Bali. He was seized by intense fear. He shared his dread with his counsellors, who included Hanuman (Maruthi, being the son of Marut, wind god; and Anjaneya, after his mother Anjana).

Hanuman, the wisest, tried to allay Sugriva's fear. Bali, who was under a curse pronounced by sage Matanga, would not come to the hill. They should not therefore be perturbed. Sugriva, who did not desire to take a chance, asked Hanuman to gauge the purpose of the strangers.

Hanuman, assuming the form of a Brahmana mendicant, sallied out. He met the princes. With his skill in expression, he addressed them in a very calm, amiable manner and enquired who they were, shedding lustre, and wielding powerful bows!

Maruthi, who closely watched their moods and gestures, explained: "Sugriva, chief of the monkeys, roamed the earth, sad and disturbed having been exiled by his brother, king Bali who ruled Kishkindha. The one in sorrow sought your friendship. I am his minister, Hanuman."

Rama was touched by the clarity of the message. He told Lakshmana the speaker sounded like one who had mastered the Vedas, observed the constraints of grammar, and controlled his words. On behalf of his brother, Lakshmana replied that they had known Sugriva's plight, and were indeed looking for him. Hanuman rejoiced.

Lakshmana, urged by Rama, told their story. Sugriva should be his brother's benefactor. He should help in the search for Sita. Gladdened in heart, Hanuman resumed his own form. He

carried the princes on his back to the presence of Sugriva. He narrated Rama's story and the events in the forest. Rama sought Sugriva's help to recover Sita. Sugriva offered his hand to be clasped by Rama in a pact of friendship. The two heroes went round a fire, which Hanuman lighted, and consecrated their alliance.

Thereafter, Sugriva told his pathetic story. He had sought refuge on the hill for fear of Bali, who had banished him. Rama, who listened intently, promised to dispose of Bali. Sugriva, for his part, solemnly pledged to find out Sita wherever she be, and help restore her to him. "Cast away grief, mighty-armed prince, I shall bring back to you the princess, Sita."

Sugriva, entering a cavern in the mountain, brought the jewels which had dropped on the hill, and which they had preserved. Holding the jewels, wrapped in Sita's raiment, Rama broke into tears. He asked Lakshmana to make sure they were Sita's ornaments. Looking at the jewels, Lakshmana said humbly, "I am not able to identify the armlets or the earrings; I recognize the anklets, for having bowed to her feet everyday!" Such was Lakshmana's rectitude!

Sugriva and Rama reaffirmed their pledges for mutual help. Those in distress forged friendship quickly.

Sugriva related the cause of his brother's hostility to him.

Bali ruled over the ancestral kingdom, Kishkindha. Sugriva remained very loyal to him. A mighty demon, Mayavi, elder brother to Dundubhi, whom Bali had killed, arrived one night at the gates of Kishkindha, roared and challenged Bali to a duel. Highly enraged, Bali emerged in fury. Out of his ineffable affection, Sugriva went with his brother. Pursued by Bali, and alarmed for life, Mayavi entered a large hole in the earth to hide. Bali pursued him entering deep into the cave, after binding Sugriva by oath to guard its opening.

Sugriva stood alert on the spot for over a year, not knowing the outcome of the duel. When blood flowed out of the hole, on account of Mayavi's magical powers, accompanied by his audacious yells, Sugriva thought Bali was killed! Stricken with grief, Sugriva blocked the mouth of the cave with a huge rock. He returned to Kishkindha. On the advice of the ministers, he installed himself king.

Having destroyed Mayavi, Bali discovered the cave closed. He was outraged. Kicking away the boulder, Bali emerged out of it. He rushed to Kishkindha. Sugriva supplicated, "You ought to forgive the offence on my part, you are the sovereign while I am ever your servant." Bali did not relent. "Your lack of wisdom is beyond forgiving," Bali said. He suspected Sugriva of treachery and banished him. Expelled, Sugriva fled and took refuge on the Rishyamuka hill.

The Rishyamuka hill was unapproachable to Bali because of the curse of sage Matanga. Bali had killed Dundubhi who had the strength of a thousand elephants. The demon had the form of a buffalo. With his single toe, Bali hurled afar his body dripping with blood, which fell in the precincts of sage Matanga's hermitage, desecrating it. The sage uttered the malediction that the one, who did the sacrilege, to die instantly on treading the Rishyamuka hill in the Matangavana. Bali knew it. The sage's curse made the hill safe for Sugriva who lived there with Hanuman and his other counsellors.

The questions that arose were puzzling! Was not Sugriva a victim of naivety? He could not have forgotten that his brother Bali was invincible in a direct encounter with an enemy—man, demon or god. Assuming Bali had died, Sugriva could have waited and fought the demon to avenge his brother's death. Did not Sugriva show a seeming hurry in assuming the kingship of Kishkindha which was Bali's? What with his unassailable prowess and merit of intense austerities, Bali for his part did not possess the quality of forgiveness!

As proof of Bali's strength Sugriva showed Rama the huge heap of Dundubhi's bones. More, seven gigantic sal trees stood having shed their leaves on being shaken by Bali, who used to wrestle with them. Sugriva tactfully enquired if Rama would be able to kill Bali in a combat. Sugriva needed proof, for his doubt was genuine in view of Bali's unmatched strength.

Smiling, and in sport, Rama lifted with his toe the carcass of Dundubhi and hurled it to a distance of ten yojanas. This put confidence in Sugriva but not fully. In order to dispel all doubts, Rama wielding his bow fitted an arrow to it and discharged it. Producing a terrible twang, the arrow pierced the seven sal trees and, shaking the forest and the nether regions, re-entered Rama's quiver!

Fully pleased, Sugriva fell at Rama's feet in acknowledgement of his extraordinary feat.

Thus assured, Sugriva accompanied by his ministers and the princes went to Kishkindha.

As the others halted behind the forest trees, Sugriva rushed to the gates of Kishkindha, raised a loud, wild roar, which was a challenge indeed! Enraged at the affront, Bali rushed out. A great combat between the brothers followed. Blinded with anger, the two fought with their palms and fists. The blows sounded like thunderbolts. Bow in hand, Rama gazed. Failing to distinguish between the twin-like forms of the brothers, Rama doubted. Pummelled, exhausted and bathed in blood, Sugriva ran and entered the forest forbidden to Bali.

Sugriva spoke piteously to Rama, "On your behest, I challenged Bali. You stood idle! Why?" Rama replied, "Bali and you resemble each other in form. I was truly puzzled. If I killed my ally, it would have been a heinous sin." On Rama's

suggestion, Lakshmana tied on Sugriva's neck a garland of flowers which distinguished him. Bali ever wore a gold chain gifted to him by his father, Lord Indra.

Sugriva, along with Rama, Lakshmana, Hanuman and other counsellors approached Kishkindha. Exhorted by Rama, Sugriva uttered a boisterous roar, challenging his brother. It shook the forest, and scared its animals and birds.

Bali heard the roar, while in his gymnasium. Never brooking a challenge, he got into a violent rage.

The poet said anger made one spiritually weak. In wrath, Bali, who shone with the splendour of gold, lost his brilliance. His eyes blazed fire. Unable to endure his brother's insolence, the monkey king stood poised to issue forth in violent hurry.

Tara, his consort, whose wisdom and affection matched her famed beauty, intervened. "Cast away this anger. Your haste fills my heart with grave fears. Sugriva, who is clever by nature, has come again, for he has obviously a powerful ally. His impudence and bravado point to that," Tara argued. Their son, prince Angada, had received the information through spies that Sugriva had contracted the friendship of Rama, prince of Ayodhya, who had come to the forest accepting exile, obeying the behest of his father. Supreme as a warrior, Rama was a repository of virtues and a refuge of the afflicted. As an alternative to a combat, Bali should invest his brother, who had formidable strength, as prince regent, and cherish him with affection. Friendship with Rama would be desirable. Anger was not a safe guide; the great hero, Bali, should not be a victim of it.

Bali acknowledged the wisdom in Tara's advice, saying "Your words hardly went wrong." Yet he reproached Tara gently. "It is my kingly duty to accept the challenge; there cannot be an alternative to that course of action. As for Rama, he is one who knew right and wrong. For your affection and advice, I pledge I shall but remove Sugriva's pride, not his life."

Tara, who had the quality of being agreeable, returned to the palace, shedding tears silently. She performed sacred rites for the king's wellbeing.

Came the second encounter. Bali, as he came out, saw his brother waiting for a fight, his eyes brimming with enmity. The clash between the heroic monkeys was unique for its terror. They grappled fiercely, their fists falling on each other in unabating fury. Blood flowed down Sugriva's huge body like a stream on the mountain slope. He tore up a sal tree and smote Bali. Between the brothers of boundless might went on a combat of a kind never before witnessed on the earth. Fighting with mountain peaks, trees, fists, and arms, they looked like a pair of contending clouds in the sky. Battered, Sugriva's eyes turned desperately in the direction of Rama.

Rama from behind a tree recognized Sugriva who wore the wild flower garland. The proper moment having come, Rama fitted to his bow a most powerful arrow and released it. Speeding like a flash of lightning, the shaft hit Bali, with resounding impact. Bali who, in a straight combat could not be subdued by anyone, was fatally assailed. In spite of his prodigious power and energy, he fell to the ground.

In the poet's words, the king richly adorned with the gold chain and other ornaments, fell like an asoka tree laden with flowers. Bali was not aware of the unseen archer.

Rama and Lakshmana approached Bali, fallen with the arrow stuck in his breast. The monkey king enquired of Rama what merit he earned by remaining hidden and striking him when he was engaged in a fierce combat! Rama of noble lineage was famed for his conduct and was therefore wrong. "Tara forbade me; yet I placed faith in your sense of honour, I showed no contumely to you. I disregarded the advice of Tara, who knew everything. Unaware of any offence to you, I have fallen. You did not face me, famed for valour as you are. As for recovering Sita, I would have had her restored to you in the course of a single day! Your contract with Sugriva to kill me was profane." Bali became mute, looking intensely at Rama.

Rama, thus reproached, replied: "You strayed from the path of virtue. An elder brother, father and teacher occupied the same position of honour." Therefore, Bali should have deemed Sugriva as his own son. On the contrary, anger made him its slave. Bali did a serious wrong, as he took his brother's wedded wife, Ruma. Being a Kshatriya, Rama upheld dharma. His deed was based on the larger law of morality.

Bali did not argue more. With tears choking his voice, Bali sought two promises: Rama should protect his son, Angada; and he should not cause humiliation to Tara who possessed exceptional virtues.

Hearing of Bali's fall at the hands of Rama, Tara, with Angada, distracted with grief, rushed to the spot. She saw Rama standing, leaning on his bow, Lakshmana and Sugriva. Hurrying past them, the proud queen clasped Bali to her bosom crying: "You spurned my advice. Death has come to you, and agony to Angada and me. Rama's feat is indeed great!" Turning to Sugriva, she said: "Your desire has been fulfilled!" Tara sat beside her husband, resolved to abstain from food and drink. Sugriva was gripped by a deep despondency.

Hanuman, sagacious and soothing of speech, tried to comfort Tara who, lying on the ground, 'shone like a star dropped from the heaven'. He suggested the performance of the funeral rites, appropriate on the occasion. "O! irreproachable lady, persuade Sugriva and Angada, who are afflicted with grief, to perform their duties."

Bali, whose life was ebbing, told Sugriva to protect Angada in

every way, like a son. "He is equal to you in prowess. What Tara says comes true, and should be done unhesitatingly." The dying hero ended: "You should keep your plighted word to Rama to recover Sita." He advised Angada to remain devoted to his uncle. He gave Sugriva his ethereal chain of gold, in which dwelt the goddess of victory. With such words of love, Bali gave up his life. The monkeys wailed, recalling Bali's celebrated deeds. Gazing on her husband's face, Tara fell to the ground, like a creeper from a huge, uprooted tree.

Nila, a general of Sugriva, pulled out the arrow from Bali's body. Tara bathed him in her tears. Angada clasped the feet of his father. Sugriva, acutely agonized, realized the folly of his antagonism. Approaching Rama, he said: "O, prince, I feel accursed. My brother was noble. He had said he wanted me to depart from Kishkindha, but would not kill me. On the contrary, I am mean to have him killed! For the misery I have caused to the noble-minded Tara and to Angada, I shall enter a blazing fire."

Disentangled from Bali's body, Tara, who beheld the lustrous form of Rama, prayed, "O, prince, kill me too, so that I go with Bali. Without me, he will be cheerless as you are without Sita." Rama, stricken with sadness, sought to comfort her, and reminded her of her duty to Angada. Thereafter Tara remained silent.

Rama asked Sugriva, Tara and the monkeys to cease wailing, for Bali attained through his prowess and steadfastness to duty his highest destiny. Sugriva, Tara and Angada performed the obsequies, with due solemnity.

Thereupon Rama asked Sugriva to assume the kingship, and to install Angada as prince regent.

An ethical question remained unanswered: Should Tara of unblemished conduct have been widowed in the effort of searching for Sita?

The month was Sravana (about July), the beginning of the rainy season. Rama and Lakshmana would remain on the mountain. When the autumnal season came in the month of Kartika (about October), Sugriva should endeavour to search for Sita.

In Kishkindha, Sugriva, joined to his wife, Ruma, became the king of the monkeys.

Rama and Lakshmana retired to a nearby cave in Prasravana, thick with trees, entwined by creepers and rich with blossoms. They could hear the music and the revelries in Kishkindha. Amidst scenes of nature's beauty, Rama spent the days and nights lost in thought of Sita. Lakshmana comforted him.

The rainy season commenced. The sky was overcast with massive clouds, which sent down rain in torrents. Lightning

lashed the sky. The dance of peacocks in the midst of sylvan cascades made the forest gay and gorgeous. The majestic elephants roamed about in rut and got startled by the rumblings of the clouds. The swarms of black bees sucked the juice of flowers. The forest abounded in trees heavily laden with fruits and dripping honey, and was rich with the music of the birds. Enjoying such rare sights, sounds and fragrance, Rama told Lakshmana that he thought of Sita. "I hope Sugriva would, on his accord, remember his obligation to recover the princess." Lakshmana shared the hope that the king of the monkeys would redeem his pledge.

Months passed, heralding the autumn season, with the sky clear and illumined with golden light.

Sugriva, living amidst luxuries, was mostly confined to his

chamber in the company of his spouse, and other beautiful women. He revelled after entrusting governance to his ministers. Given to excessive enjoyments, he hardly noticed the change of season. Hanuman, who ever knew what ought to be done, tactfully reminded the king of his obligation to Rama. "Let the commitment be honoured."

Sugriva, who took the hint, commanded Nila, to summon and gather the monkey troops in all quarters. The king relapsed into a life of pleasure.

Meanwhile, Rama dwelling on Prasravana felt agonized through memory of Sita. The time fixed for beginning the search for Sita after the rains lapsed. Viewing the sky glowing and resonant with the cries of birds, Rama was tormented by pangs of love. He spoke to Lakshmana: "Autumn has set in with its loveliness reflected in all aspects of nature. Where is Sita? Has the king become a slave of carnal pleasures, and forgot his duty?" Seeing Rama in distress, Lakshmana got disturbed. Anger rose in him. Rama spoke to his brother gently suggesting to avoid harsh words, yet to remind Sugriva who was bound by his oath.

Bearing his bow, Lakshmana proceeded to Kishkindha. In spite of his self-possession, he was moved by righteous anger. The monkeys on the way fled. Lakshmana commanded prince Angada, who was perturbed, to inform Sugriva of his arrival, tormented by the plight of his brother. Angada rushed to the king who slept drunk with wine and infatuated with sensual pleasures. Waking up, Sugriva heard the submission of Angada. "Remain true to your promise," reminded his thoughtful counsellors.

Sugriva readily accepted his obligation to Rama, whose deed was beyond repayment. Hanuman was articulate. "Lakshmana's coming has a meaning and Rama needed to be pleased. The understanding with him should be fulfilled."

In the company of Angada, Lakshmana entered the city and went to the royal palace which stood amidst beautiful groves, mansions with lofty pinnacles and protected by many enclosures. He entered the large gynaeceum decked with flowers and jewels and filled with music and lively with beautiful ladies. Not assuaged by these, Lakshmana in his vehemence twanged his bow.

The monkey king, who heard the terrible sound, was alarmed. Cautious as ever, he advised Tara, of rare comeliness and conduct, to greet Lakshmana. Going to Lakshmana, Tara spoke in choicest words suggesting he ought to bear with even negligence on the part of Sugriva. For, even as he was lost in the gratification of his senses, he remained a true friend conscientious in the discharge of his duty to Rama. The soothing words had their effect on Lakshmana's mind. Watching the softening in the prince, Tara mentioned that Sugriva had indeed embarked on his effort and a vast number of monkeys with extraordinary might had arrived from the mountains.

On the request of Tara, Lakshmana proceeded to Sugriva who, seated on a couch of gold, was surrounded by all manner of splendour. The king stood up with folded hands, his spouse, Ruma, beside him.

Lakshmana yet disturbed, said to the king: "Honour your pledge to my brother. Bali is gone, beware of such peril!"

Tara, famed for her dignity and tact, assured Lakshmana that Sugriva was not perfidious. Having gained the kingdom, he gave himself to excessive happiness, and remained oblivious of the passage of time. The lapse in the circumstances should be pardoned. A noble prince as he was, he should not give himself to anger. For accomplishing the mission, messengers had gone to all quarters to bring innumerable monkeys of vast prowess whom the king would employ. Sugriva would ensure reunion of

Rama and Sita. Receiving the assurance, Lakshmana was
partly pacified.

Calling Hanuman, Sugriva entrusted to him the task of
summoning the hordes of monkeys, bears, baboons from all
directions.

The monkeys started arriving from the Himalaya, Kailasa,
Mandara, Mahendra, Dhumra, Vindhya, Meru and other
mountain ranges, forests, and seashores including the ocean of
milk. They rushed to Kishkindha carrying roots, fruits and
herbs and flowers to offer to their sovereign.

Meanwhile, Sugriva, along with Lakshmana, proceeded to the

presence of Rama. He stood with joined palms, and then fell at his feet. Rama suggested that the task of tracing out Sita should be taken on hand. On orders of the king, the monkeys in crores came into view. Many had extraordinary forms such as Satabali, Susena, Kesari, Gavaksa and Dhumra. The troop commanders included Nila, who stood like a heap of antimony, Gavaya, who shone like a mountain of gold, Darimukha, Mainda, Vinata, Gaja, Dwivida, Jambavan, Rumana, Gandhamadana, Angada, Durmukha, Nala, Sarabha, Kumuda, Vahni, Rambha and many more. Having paraded the monkey leaders, Sugriva sought orders from Rama.

Much pleased, Rama suggested the first task was to secure proof of Sita being alive. The land where Ravana lived should be found out. The directions in which the search was to be made, and the leaders of monkeys given the respective tasks were decided carefully. A troop leader, Vinata, was asked to explore the eastern quarter with its mountains, forests and woods. The region included Javadwipa (island of Java), and beyond. The western quarter was assigned to Susena, the northern quarter to Satabali, each assisted by powerful monkeys. The southern region was assigned to heroes including Nila, Hanuman, Jambavan, Gavaksa, Gavaya, Mainda, Dwivida, Gandhamadana. It was headed by prince Angada.

The king set one month to complete the task of discovering Sita. That was a deadline not to be broken!

Sugriva addressed Hanuman. Neither on earth nor in air nor in the sky nor in waters did exist obstruction to Maruthi's movement. His might and adroitness too were similar to those of wind god. He was endowed with unique discretion. He could perform the given task for he possessed tact, strength, wisdom, prowess, conformability to place and time and, above all, prudence.

Rama, who had observed Hanuman's conduct, his mind full of affection, esteem and hope, handed over to the son of wind god the signet ring, inscribed with his name. He said, "Seeing this ring, Sita will accept you to have arrived from me. Your strength, resolution and courage, as also the words of Sugriva, will accomplish the purpose." Taking the ring reverentially, Hanuman tucked it on his head, and bowed at Rama's feet. Rama blessed him. Hanuman set forth, with joined palms, in the southern direction, accompanied by the generals; the troops of monkeys followed them. The monkeys assigned to the other directions sallied forth roaring, vying with one another in confidence and speed. Sugriva, having despatched the monkeys, felt gratified.

Rama and Lakshmana lived on mount Prasravana with deep concern.

The monkeys proceeding south explored the whole region, its caves, rivers and forests. They circumambulated the Vindhya mountains. Going into a deep cave, they saw a woman ascetic clad in bark and black antelope skin, effulgent with glory. She was Swayamprabha. Hanuman sought her help in their mission. The woman, using the power of her asceticism, transported the monkeys out of the cave and indicated the direction to the southern sea. She blessed them. They hastened south.

The monkeys saw at a distance the southern waters, with their roaring billows. They despaired. Angada reminded them that the time limit set by the king had slipped away! Vehement by nature, Sugriva would not forgive them. Death was sure to befall them. Therefore, their death at that place was preferable. The monkeys sat down on the kusa grass with their heads pointing towards the south. They roared in despair.

Hearing the uproar, Sampathi, king of vultures, emerged from a mountain cave. He heard from the monkeys the story of Rama,

and the death of his brother, Jatayu. Sampathi said his brother was dearer to him than his life itself. He was highly gratified with the praises uttered by the monkeys.

Wingless Sampathi told his story. Seeking to conquer Indra, Jatayu and Sampathi flew to the heaven. Drawing near the sun, Jatayu began to be tormented by the sun's rays. Fearing danger, Sampathi covered his brother with his own wings. His wings burnt, Sampathi dropped down on the Vindhya range.

Angada enquired if Sampathi knew the abode of Ravana. Sampathi mentioned he had heard a young lady crying out, 'O, Rama, O, Lakshmana!' while being borne away by Ravana. She had great splendour. Ravana's island kingdom, Lanka, lay

a hundred yojanas from the shore. It was constructed by
Viswakarma, architect of the gods. There sits Sita. Using his
supersensuous vision, he saw Sita in seclusion in Lanka.

Sampathi was taken to the sea, as he desired, where he offered
prayers for the spirit of Jatayu. His virtuous act for Rama was
destined. The recovery of his wings would be an assurance of
success in the search of the monkeys. Large wings grew on the
bird, who rose into the air majestically as the monkeys watched
in amazement. The monkeys, who roared in joy, leapt towards
the shore of the southern sea.

The sea was both calm and turbulent. While the monkeys felt
despondent, Angada took counsel with the elders. 'An endeavour

that lacks spirit fails.' Their mission should not.

The troop leaders proclaimed their leaping ability. One could leap ten yojanas, others twenty yojanas, thirty yojanas, forty yojanas, sixty yojanas, seventy yojanas, eighty yojanas, ninety yojanas. Finally, Jambavan said that in earlier days he could leap more than a hundred yojanas. He had circled the earth when God Vishnu in his Vamana (Brahmana Dwarf) incarnation grew to measure the universe in three strides.

Angada could surely leap over. Jambavan observed shrewdly, "The task was for others; and not for one who led the expedition. The ethics and strategy needed the prince regent to remain behind." The ruling on conduct uttered by Jambavan had wisdom of ages.

Jambavan addressed Hanuman, who had sat apart quietly, "The son of wind god is equal to Garuda for strength and speed." He reminded Hanuman of his parentage. There was a celestial nymph, Punjikasthala. Owing to a curse by a rishi, she was reborn as Anjana to a monkey chief, Kunjara. To her was born, through wind god, Maruthi, with extraordinary energy. Jambavan recalled his childhood feat of leaping three thousand yojanas into the sky to swallow the sun, his having been hurt by the thunderbolt hurled by Lord Indra, hence Hanuman (lit. one with hurt chin), and the boon of invulnerability in combat God Brahma bestowed on him. He could grow beyond bounds.

So reminded, Hanuman recalled his strength. He expanded his form to an immense size. He became conscious of his ability to leap over the ocean. "I shall see Sita," he assured. Seeing Hanuman growing into an immeasurable form and hearing his heroic words, the monkeys rejoiced. They prayed for the success of the mission.

Hanuman ascended the mountain Mahendra, and assumed a yogic pose to spring into the air. The mountain soared with high peaks bearing fruits, flowers, and thick with animals, birds and serpents. Under Maruthi's feet, it screamed, the rocks disintegrated throwing up springs of water, and shaking huge trees causing the birds to fly, and the wild animals to run in alarm. The serpents, ejected from their holes, remained poised in the air.

Standing composed, and possessing the speed of wind, the blessed monkey, enshrined Rama and Sita in his thought, for betaking himself across the sea to Lanka.

SUNDARA KANDA

Discovery Of Sita

The kanda is 'sundara' (beautiful) for its poetry; it is beautiful for the discovery of Sita (truth) bringing happiness to Rama; it is beautiful for marvels of the deeds of Hanuman.

With his head thrust forward, in solemn earnestness, his palms joined in prayer to his progenitor, wind god, and his mind centred on Rama's purpose, Hanuman stood poised to leap over the ocean.

The monkeys gazed at him in wonder.

The hero pressed the mountain with his hands and feet. The mountain shook, the trees shed their flowers. Water gushed up, letting loose streams reflecting the lustre of gold, silver and antimony as they flowed through layers of minerals. Massive boulders fell and rocks split. The animals in the caverns shrieked, and the birds of all kinds created a clamour. Spitting

venom, the serpents, that were provoked, hit the rocks and raised their heads. Flames of fire leaped up. The inhabitants of the mountain such as the vidyadharas (adept in knowledge, spells) with hosts of their womenfolk enjoying life there, charanas (celestial bards) and siddhas (semi-divine beings) left, hovering in the air.

Hanuman quivered and thundered like a massive cloud. While about to spring, he stretched out his tail, and curled it high. Summoning his full energy, courage and vividly casting his eyes upwards as if to measure the distance, and controlling his breath, he stood assuring the monkeys: "As an arrow loosed by Rama, I shall course to Lanka."

Hanuman rose into the sky. The impact was terrific. In the poet's words, the uprooted trees laden with blossoms thrust forward, like noble hosts accompanying an honoured guest for a little distance to see him off, and they fell back into the sea. The flowers spread on the waters, the sea looked like the firmament spangled with innumerable stars.

Hanuman moved in space, his image falling on the sea. The wind that was set in motion by his passage threw up huge billows. The creatures in the sea got tossed up. As Hanuman bounded apace like a winged mountain, the celestials rained flowers on him. Wind god refreshed his son who was pursuing Rama's purpose. The rishis extolled him, and the gandharvas and the yakshas lauded Rama's messenger.

As desired by Varuna, sea god, Minaka mountain emerging from the ocean-bed rose to offer hospitality to Hanuman: "O, son of wind god, you are worthy of such honour." Deeply imbued with his resolve, Hanuman replied: "I should not halt midway in my mission." And touching the mountain with his head in courtesy, Hanuman sped on higher through the cloudless sky. The gods and the rishis lauded Hanuman's concentration on his task.

Surasa, mother of the serpents, assumed an enormous and hideous form, with her huge mouth, and stood in the path of Hanuman. She asked him to enter her mouth for her food. Hanuman replied he would oblige her after completing his duty to Rama. "None dare elude me," so saying the ogress blocked the path, opening her mouth wider. Provoked, Hanuman asked Surasa to widen her mouth so as to take him. He grew into ten yojanas in size; Surasa widened her mouth to twenty yojanas. They vied with each other until Surasa stood with her mouth gaping a hundred yojanas, as wide as the sea! Lo, Hanuman, reduced himself in an instant to the size of a thumb; he shot through Surasa's mouth and emerged instantly through her ear!

Thwarted, yet highly pleased, Surasa blessed Hanuman to fulfil the purpose of Rama. The gods and all, who watched the

encounter, marvelled at Maruthi's wit and prowess.

Seeing Hanuman speeding like Garuda, an ogress Simhika, with magical powers, clutched Hanuman's shadow from below. Hanuman wondered! Looking down he saw the huge dark form. With a body as hard and sharp as diamond, Hanuman tore through her, making the creature fall in fragments on the ocean waves.

All living beings looked on the speeding messenger in amazement.

Spanning the ocean, Hanuman still hovering in the air, saw Lanka girt by the sea. Reflecting, he contracted his form to his natural one. He was one who had 'mastered' himself! He descended. Hanuman perceived Lanka, perched on the summit of the Trikuta mountain.

Hanuman surveyed Lanka, by passing amidst hills, and dark, green meadows, forests and groves full of flowers, fruits and fragrance. The city was protected by moats. Demons armed with terrible weapons ranged on every side. A golden wall with magnificent gateways encircled the city, which was crowded with lofty buildings flaunting flags and pennons, and hemmed in with pathways. Lying on the summit of the mountain, Lanka looked like a dream city in the air.

Reaching the northern gate, Hanuman became thoughtful. The city was fully guarded. He reflected, 'messengers given to bravado could bring to nought serious undertakings'. Rama's cause should not be stultified. He decided to enter the city during night.

The night having come, Hanuman reduced himself to the size of a cat. Springing up in every stride, he viewed the pathways amidst the dwellings, mansions with golden pillars, archways studded with diamonds and crystals that shone brightly in the moonlit night. Standing on the peak of a hill, Hanuman looked with wonder on the city. With its sights and sounds, and aligned symmetrically, Lanka was a delight to the senses. It was resonant with soulful music.

Hanuman leapt up the defence wall. Approaching the gateway, he saw an ogress of fierce form guarding it. Emitting a loud cry, she challenged, "Who are you, monkey, and what motive has brought you here? I am Lanka-Sri, the embodied glory of the city. I guard it."

Hanuman, in turn, questioned her. The ogress uttering a frightful cry, struck Hanuman forcefully. Growing into a huge size, Hanuman smote her with his mighty hard-clenched fist that fell like a mount of diamond. Receiving the overpowering blow, Lanka-Sri precipitately fell to the ground. Seeing her prostrated, Hanuman showed compassion due to a woman. She

admired Hanuman's strength which vanquished her. The prophecy of God Brahma came true: 'When you are subdued by a monkey of terrible might and merit, know that the destruction of Ravana and all the ogres has arrived.' "Therefore, accomplish your purpose," she said. Lanka-Sri departed, and with her the glory of Lanka.

In the city Hanuman searched in all places. He heard melodious songs of varying notes. He heard the tinkling of ornaments and anklets of women, and the roar of heroes. He listened to the uttering of sacred texts and the Vedas. Songs eulogised the might of Ravana. Many were engaged in yogic practices as anchorites and recluses. Many wore various kinds of weapons, and assumed diverse forms.

Ravana's palace stood amidst the fabulous mansions on the summit of Trikuta. Moats adorned with white lotuses girdled it.

The gynaeceum was resonant with marvellous sounds, and noisy with the neighing of horses, the movements of chariots, and aerial cars. Elephants and powerful demons guarded it.

At night, the island kingdom lay bathed in moonlight. The rakshasas gave themselves to joyous abandon. Women and their spouses slept blissfully, as also violent ogres and ogresses disporting themselves. Women of rare beauty shone like flashes of lightning. Amidst all these, Hanuman missed Sita! Ranging over the city, Hanuman approached Ravana's palace, which was enclosed by a dazzling wall displaying figures drawn in molten silver, with archways decked with ornaments of gold. It had planned, concentric enclosures and charming gateways. Mounted elephants and unwearied horses, and marvellous chariots stood by. Mansions of great car-warriors dominated the scene. Mighty ogres thronged on every side.

Hanuman, who observed all details keenly, leapt on from mansion to mansion. He saw the houses of Prahasta,

Mahaparswa, Kumbhakarna and Vibhishana, among others, and of Indrajit. He saw wonderful buildings with picture galleries, and pleasure houses. Amidst all these, Hanuman identified Ravana's abode. He entered the palace.

It comprised many mansions, with lattices of gold inlaid with cat's-eye gems, looking like a mass of clouds pierced by lightning. It was of incomparable aura. The aerial car, Pushpaka, stood by. Studded with gems and jewels, it had a lotus pond within it, with exquisite figures carved around it. Leaping up Pushpaka, which served as vantage point, Hanuman gazed on Ravana's chamber, which had a high dais made of crystal and precious stones. Lights burned from lamps of gold. The chamber was ablaze with brilliance. The dais had a canopy with gorgeous wreaths. Around it stood women fanning, with whisks. Fragrance of perfumes and incense filled the chamber.

Hanuman saw the form of Ravana. On an upholstered bed adorned with flowers, lay the many-armed Ravana. He was clad in robes of golden hue, and adorned with precious ornaments. The sight was startling.

Hanuman looked intently on Ravana, who lay sleeping. Ravana's body bore auspicious marks. His face was lit up by his flaming earrings. Each head of his bore a diadem of gold. His chest was broad and mighty. Lying in close proximity were his many spouses, some in poses displaying the dancing moods, and some holding the musical instruments. On Ravana's flank lay on a magnificent couch his consort, Mandodari, whose beauty illuminated the chamber.

Hanuman, who was exceptionally conscientious, searched the entire gynaeceum of Ravana. He did not find Sita!

The assiduous messenger continued the search. His mood turned into one of hope, then one of despair. He brooded. Could Ravana have killed Sita?

The monkey scoured pools, ponds, lakes, streams, rivers, forest regions and hills. 'Sampathi had located Sita in Lanka! Yet I do not perceive her anywhere! Should my effort come to naught? How would noble Rama bear the loss?' He had a choice—to destroy Ravana himself or carry him as captive across the sea and lay him at the feet of Rama.

Having reflected thus, Hanuman recollected his endless prowess and energy for persistence. He contemplated searching in Ravana's favourite asoka grove. He invoked the blessings of the gods for his success.

Hanuman entered the famed grove. He felt thrilled in his limbs and in his mind, which he considered auspicious. He surveyed the grove, with the trees in blossom and rendered noisy by birds, and stirred by the movements of deer and other animals.

He penetrated deep into it. The flowers that fell from the trees covered him as if welcoming him! The gorgeous garden lay in jubilant disarray as if to receive an esteemed guest who had arrived.

A singular asoka tree, embellished by clusters of climbers, and surrounded on all sides by golden daisies, attracted Hanuman's attention. At a close distance stood a temple, with steps of coral, and in it he caught sight of a woman sitting surrounded by many ogres. Though emaciated, she had splendour. Clad in soiled yellow clothes, she looked like 'a flame enveloped by smoke'. She sighed again and again. Her face was bathed in tears. Hanuman leapt up the asoka tree, and remained unseen amidst its branches. So positioned, he watched the events.

Hanuman guessed the distressed lady to be Sita! He gazed on Sita's noble form, recalling the lady who was being carried away by Ravana. She wore the same ornaments on her limbs as Rama had described. Her eyes resembled the petals of a lotus. The ornaments of sapphire on her neck cast a bluish radiance around. She had a slender waist with well-formed limbs and features. The poet compared the unique form of Sita, as seen by Hanuman, to perfection impeded by grief. Sita looked around like a frightened fawn. Hanuman concluded 'this was Sita, for whose sake Rama's mind was in torment, going through pity, tenderness, grief and love. The beauty and elegance and composure of Sita equalled those of Rama.' The son of wind god meditated on Rama, invoking his blessings.

The chanting of the Vedas and other sacred texts marked the end of the night. Awakened by the strains of music, Ravana thought of Sita. Passion possessed him. Adorned with rare apparels and ornaments, he entered the asoka grove. Many women followed him, some bearing torches, others carrying chowries and fans, some with water in golden ewers and with pitchers made of jewels filled with wine. The giant moved under a canopy resembling a swan. Hanuman saw Ravana, who had accomplished unparalleled deeds. He was full of vanity, with eyes intoxicated with infatuation. He moved with a grand gait.

Hanuman looked with wonder on the glory of the suzerain lord of the rakshasas. He watched intently.

As Ravana drew near, Sita shook in fear. Huddled up, she shed tears from her large reddish eyes, absorbed in devotion to Rama.

Ravana, with his twenty eyes, gazed on Sita. He spoke eloquently about his many-faceted glory, to impress Sita: "There is no woman, who is comparable in comeliness to you. Your fidelity to Rama is a folly. There is none in the universe who would match me in might and virility. You should become my foremost queen. Your husband in exile will not be able to regain you. Rama is no equal to me in might, glory, even in asceticism."

Sita, stricken with grief, sat absorbed in the thoughts of Rama.

When Ravana finished, Sita placed a straw between her and the demon king, and addressed it. "Withdraw your mind from me. Follow the course of conduct of the virtuous. The fickle man brings affluent kingdoms and cities to ruin. Lanka will before long perish for the fault of one, yourself. I am undivided from Rama, as sunlight is from the sun. When enraged, he is peerless in prowess. Rama, with Lakshmana, will take away your life as the sun sucks up the shallow water."

Hearing the words, Ravana uttered the warning. He had set a limit of twelve months for his waiting. Two more months remained. If she did not agree to be his spouse, she would serve as his morsel of food.

Sita, firm of mind, said, "Your conduct was reproachful. None in the three worlds would antagonize Rama. If the fire of my purity did not reduce you to ashes, it was because I did not have Rama's consent. There was no heroism in carrying me away through guile. It was a device ordained by fate to bring about your destruction."

Sita's words made Ravana's eyes roll in rage. His diadems shook. With a mind seized with passion, he roared, and commanded the women to bend Sita's will in his favour. Thereafter Ravana left the grove. The rakshasa women menaced and, in turn, coaxed Sita. Hanuman watched silently.

Sita lamented, calling the name of Rama and Lakshmana. She wondered why her lord had not so far rescued her. Did not Rama meet Jatayu, who fought Ravana? she wondered. If he knew where she was, he would have churned up the ocean and reduced Lanka to ashes. Death was preferable to a life removed from Rama.

Seeing Sita intimidated by the women around her, an aged ogress Trijata, who had woken from her sleep, described a dream she had. Sitting on a palanquin of celestial glory, Rama and Lakshmana, clad in white, came to Lanka. Sita was united with Rama. Ravana, attired in red, was pulled in a chariot drawn by asses. Lanka lay shattered. Trijata asked the demonesses to cease harassing Sita.

Having watched the happenings keenly, Hanuman was satisfied he had succeeded in his mission! Yet he should reassure the agonized princess; otherwise he would be blameworthy. Overdoing should however be avoided. A wrong action on the part of a messenger would be a serious error.

Hanuman, who perched amid the boughs, began narrating the story of Rama. Extremely clear in speech, he described the events briefly and in chosen words. "In search of Sita, Rama met Sugriva. Having killed the mighty Bali, Rama placed Sugriva on the throne, and at the latter's command, thousands upon thousands of monkeys spread out in all directions to discover Sita. Sampathi saw her. Therefore, I leaped a hundred yojanas across the ocean in search of the long-eyed lady. I have found her, who in comeliness and beauty answers Rama's description of her." Completing the story, the messenger fell silent.

Sita, hearing the heroic events, was struck with supreme wonder. Turning her face, she looked up into the boughs enquiringly. Her peering eyes saw the flashing amidst the boughs. The simian's eyes shone bright as refined gold. His posture was one of humility. Suspecting the sight to be possibly an illusion, Sita fainted. Waking, she cried, 'Rama'.

Hanuman descended softly. Distracted with fear, Sita reflected and prayed that what she heard be true!

Standing in front of Sita, bowing down with his joined palms, the messenger spoke guardedly, "Pray, who are you?

O, lady of rare beauty, if you are Sita, consort of Rama carried away by Ravana from Janasthana, reveal it to me."

Thrilled by the name of Rama, Sita told her own story, concluding that if she was not rescued within two more months, she would be killed by Ravana. Hanuman answered he had come as an envoy of Rama. Lakshmana, tormented with grief, saluted her with his head bent low. Sita, who still had lingering fear of deception, sat with her eyes downcast. Asked by Sita, Hanuman gave a full description of Rama, his strength, grace, and qualities.

Gauging Sita's mood, Hanuman spoke assuringly that Rama, Lakshmana, and Sugriva with his vast monkey army, had joined to discover and rescue Sita. He was one of them. He was Hanuman, son of wind god.

Yet cautious, Sita made Hanuman to repeat Rama's story, made him describe Rama and Lakshmana, and their bodily features. "I am famed for my exploits. I have recounted the story to inspire confidence in you."

Sita shed tears of joy. Hanuman gave her Rama's ring with his name inscribed on it. Seeing her lord's signet ring, Sita's face shone with joy. She praised Hanuman for his valour, wisdom, and fearlessness. Hanuman told Sita that Rama, accompanied by the army of monkeys, would instantly come, on hearing his report. He would destroy Ravana and recover her.

Sita, with grief gone, got grieved over Rama's sorrow. The news of Rama, who was given over to agony, was like 'nectar mixed with poison'. "Rama of unequal prowess should rescue me soon," Sita insisted.

Seeing Sita's anxiety, Hanuman said with a rare tinge of humour that he could restore her to Rama at once; if she perched on his back, he could leap over the ocean to Rama; indeed he could carry the whole Lanka.

Even as Sita felt enthused, she said that Hanuman's proposal was typically 'monkeylike'! "You are so diminutive of form!" Hearing Sita's remark, which none else had dared to make, Hanuman grew into a terrible size resembling a mountain. He reassured her he could carry the entire Lanka with Ravana on his back.

That settled Sita's mind. Yet, exercising tact, which a virtuous lady observed, she said her being carried by Hanuman at great speed over the sea was hazardous; for other reasons also it was not proper. Totally devoted to Rama, she would not touch on her own free will the body of anyone other than her lord! Therefore, Hanuman should bring to her Rama with speed.

Anjaneya admired Sita's modesty and firmness, which went with her noble character.

The messenger asked Sita for a token by means of which Rama could know that he had for certain seen her. Sita confided in him an incident that took place in the forest near the Chitrakoot mount and which Rama and she alone knew—laceration of her breasts by a vicious crow while Rama slept in her arms, and how a blade of grass charged with divine potency released by Rama chased the bird as it roamed everywhere and destroyed its right eye! Sita, taking her jewel (choodamani) which she wore on her hair, gave it to Hanuman to be delivered to Rama.

Receiving the jewel, Hanuman walked round Sita in reverence, and stood with head bent low by her side. Troubled by a lingering doubt, Sita said, "You are indeed mighty and can cross the sea. But how can the horde of monkeys accomplish this task?"

Hanuman answered with his characteristic tact and self-possession that there were in Sugriva's command many monkeys who were his equals and superior to him. "Surely, such ones are not sent on errands as I was. They would come with Rama and Lakshmana." Sita admired Hanuman's modesty, and granted him leave to depart, with her blessing. He carried her message for Rama: 'Beyond a month I am not going to survive in your absence, O, prince!'

Hanuman thought deeply—a small fraction of his duty remained. This was to give Ravana a foretaste of the might of Rama and of the monkeys! He decided to lay waste Ravana's excellent grove, which compared to Lord Indra's Nandanavana.

The son of wind god assumed a huge forbidding form and, with furious energy, he set to work. He divested Ravana's pleasure garden, reducing it to a jumble. He uprooted trees, churned up ponds making them muddy, and crushed hills. The animals and birds shrieked in distress. The lovely creepers displaced looked 'like women with their robes in disarray'. The asoka grove, Ravana's enchanting garden became a jumble, amidst which Hanuman blazed with martial glory.

The ogres fled to report the devastation to Ravana. "The

exception is the place where stood the asoka tree under which Sita sits," they said. Listening to the report of vandalism, Ravana flared up like a 'funeral fire'. On his orders kinkaras (attendants), departed to capture the monkey.

A large number of them sallied forth. Approaching the archway, where Hanuman had placed himself joyously, they assailed the intruder with maces, iron bludgeons and arrows, spears, pikes, lances, javelins. Uttering an audacious cry, Hanuman swished his long tail and lashed the ground, the sound of which filled Lanka. He shouted, "Victory to Rama and Lakshmana and to Sugriva. I am Rama's servant!"

Attacked from all sides, Hanuman swept through the air, felled the rakshasas. Raining mighty blows, he stood athirst for combat. A few demons, who survived, ran and reported to Ravana the phenomenal happening.

Ravana commanded Jambumali, son of his minister Prahasta, to engage the monkey. Meanwhile, Hanuman toppled the edifice of the sanctuary. The sound of the crash reverberated in Lanka. He gave out a thunder-like roar, causing terror to the demons. The infuriated messenger impetuously tore up a pillar decked with gold and bristling with a hundred edges and spun it around which, as it collided with other pillars, caused fire. The whole edifice got ablaze.

Jambumali, ferocious, and adorned with a garland of red flowers sallied forth.

The demon roared, Hanuman too roared. The giant attacked Hanuman with arrows on the archway. Stained with blood, Hanuman's celebrated countenance looked 'like a large blown lotus illuminated by a sunbeam in autumn'. Waxing in wrath, he tore up a giant rock and hurled it at Jambumali, who broke it with his arrows. A sal tree met the same fate. Finding the demon to be of unusual might, Hanuman seized the ogre's iron club; hurled with violent anger, it shattered Jambumali's body, his head and arms, his weapons, chariot and armaments. The rakshasa fell in fragments.

Likewise, Hanuman destroyed many such heroic demons. He killed five more generals despatched by Ravana, including Yupeksha, Durdhara and Bhaskarna. Hanuman stood victorious on the archway.

Hearing the massacre, Ravana, who sat in the assembly, sent his son Aksha to confront the monkey. Rash by nature, and armed with various weapons, and wearing a bright princely armour, riding in his decorated chariot yoked to eight horses, Aksha advanced fast to the archway. The cries of elephants, horses and the rattling of large chariots filled the air as they approached Hanuman, who gazed on the prince with an 'eye full of regard', and reflecting on his own strength.

Aksha pierced Hanuman with whetted shafts. These proving ineffective, he provoked Hanuman to an encounter. Fiery of spirit, Aksha met Hanuman at close quarters. It was a great fight. Rejoicing, Hanuman grew in size and Aksha's arrows fell like the rain pouring on a mountain. Thundering, he sprang into the air. He reflected on the prowess of the prince, which grew in combat. 'Putting an end to him, therefore, finds favour with me. A spreading fire is not worth neglecting.' Thus pondering, Hanuman killed the horses and broke the chariot of Aksha. The latter bounded into the air, with his bow and sword. Meeting the prince, Hanuman caught him, and dashed him violently to the ground. Aksha fell to the earth's surface, his limbs and body crushed and shattered. The celestials looked astonished at the feat.

Hearing of the astounding event, Ravana commanded Indrajit (alias Meghanada lit. sound of cloud), his elder son, who had made Lord Indra captive, to proceed to slay Hanuman.

Indrajit, brimming with martial ardour, rushed forth in his chariot, yoked to four steeds, and drove to the enemy. Hearing the rattling of Indrajit's chariot and the twang of his bowstring, Hanuman rejoiced. Curious about the outcome of the confrontation between the two invincible heroes, the celestials filled the sky. Watching Indrajit's advance, Hanuman grew to immense proportions. Indrajit, full of passion for war, and the son of wind god unequalled in encounter, closed on each other. Amidst the rumblings of his chariot, and the crack of war-drums, Indrajit, rained arrows from his marvellous bow. Maruthi, swift as wind, baffled his marksmanship. The poet said the battle 'captivated the minds of all created beings'.

Wheeling amidst the arrows around him, the monkey remained unscathed. Indrajit gave way to despair. He would capture the monkey, whom his weapons could not assail, he thought. Indrajit fitted to his bow the missile presided over by God Brahma, and released it. Swift thoughts ran through Hanuman's mind. He needed to show deference to the divine weapon. He recalled the boon bestowed on him by the Creator that he would be freed even from the bondage of the missile after a brief while, and any more bond put on him would remove the missile's efficacy! Hanuman bowed to the cosmic weapon, reflecting 'my passing bondage would give me an opportunity to meet Ravana'. Hanuman, assailed by the Brahmastra, sank to the ground.

The demons took hold of Hanuman, who ceased all movement, bound him with sturdy ropes. With the binding, the potency of the Brahmastra ceased. Hanuman was free. Hanuman, for his part, pretended to be unaware of his freedom!

He permitted himself to be dragged by the warriors to Ravana's presence.

In the assembly hall, Hanuman saw Ravana enthroned, with demons sitting at his feet. The king shone with rich energy, his coppery eyes rolling in rage. Commanded by the king, Prahasta, queried the monkey who he was, how he came to Lanka, and what his intention was.

Hanuman looked intensely on Ravana, whose power and glory impressed him, and replied with serene calm. He was in the service of Sugriva, the monkey king, brother of Bali and had arrived on a mission of Rama, son of Dasaratha. The purpose caused him to leap over the sea, and brought him to Lanka. He said: "Surrender Sita to Rama which would be a righteous conduct for you inasmuch as Sita is indeed death itself. Rama is invincible!"

Hearing the nonchalant admonition, Ravana was beside himself with anger. He ordered the death of the intrepid intruder. As the ministers and attendants stood in awe,

Vibhishana counselled: "O, brother, your learning and knowledge have endowed you with excellent judgement. We should not act wrongly. The stranger is a messenger, and his killing is neither ordained by the scriptures nor sanctioned by ethics. An envoy does not merit death. You could punish him, if you so desire."

Accepting the advice Ravana decided to punish Hanuman. He ordered to set his tail on fire: "Let him return deformed." Obeying the command, the attendants began to wrap Hanuman's tail in cotton rags. While they were in the act, the tail lengthened enormously, causing despair in the minds of the rakshasas. As his tail was being swathed, the son of wind god grew out of all proportions. His tail grew without end! Soaking the tail with oil, in evil glee, the demons set fire to Maruthi's tail. He lay quiet enjoying the situation. As they started to stir, he smote the henchmen with his long, powerful blazing tail. The women folk, children and the aged, who saw the sight, were filled with delight.

Hanuman pondered: 'I am beyond reprisal by Rama's enemies. For his pleasure, I shall suffer humiliation.' He calculated that as the rakshasas carried him from place to place, he could survey Lanka, its fortifications, and defence structures. With blasts of conches, beating of kettle drums, Ravana's servants merrily hauled Hanuman through Lanka. Hanuman, who observed keenly, got a good idea of the layout of Lanka, its mansions, quadrangles, crossroads, streets and lanes and sequestered tracts. The denizens of Lanka looked with delight on the procession.

The women, who attended on Sita, informed her of the happenings. Deeply concerned, she prayed in the name of her virtue to fire god to prove cool to Hanuman. The fire, which had started raging, turned mild on the tail of the son of

wind god! The wind blew ice-cold around Hanuman, who understood the mercy of Sita, the compassion of his father, and the glory of Rama.

Shrinking his form in a trice, Hanuman cast off his bonds, and leapt into the air, giving a terrible shout. Passing over the mansions, he scattered blazing fire over Ravana's palace. He burnt the palace of Indrajit, of Kumbhakarna, and of Jambumali, Sumali, among others. He spared the palace of Vibhishana. Like a cloud charged with lightning, he flitted over the mansions and pleasances. The structures collapsed amidst fantastic cries and sounds. Fire raged, with the help of wind, and enveloped the whole of Lanka. Having accomplished the incredible feat, Hanuman sought in mind Rama's benediction. The gods, vidyadharas and gandharvas watched the burning of Lanka with joy.

Hanuman leapt to the sea and quenched the fire on his tail. Seeing the city of Lanka blazing, Hanuman became thoughtful. 'Blessed are those who curb anger. Woe to me, who did not think of the safety of Sita!' While so pondering, he heard about the miraculous protection of Sita. Joy filled his soul. He wondered how Sita had escaped destruction. Hanuman decided to visit her, to be sure. He leapt to the grove where Sita sat.

Hanuman saw Sita, ensconced at the foot of the asoka tree. She gazed fondly on Hanuman, who again assured her of his return with Rama, Lakshmana and the monkey army for her restoration. Having comforted her, the messenger took leave of Sita.

Hanuman ascended the Arisba peak on Trikuta mountain, which heaved under his weight as he grew in size. He sprang into the air across the sea, tearing asunder masses of clouds. Sighting mount Mahendra, Hanuman emitted a roar like thunder lashing his tail. "Seen have I Sita," he shouted. The monkeys, who had waited most eagerly, heard it and jumped in explosive joy. Hanuman descended on top of the mountain. The delighted monkeys gathered around him with roots, fruits, flowers and boughs of trees.

Hanuman saluted the elders and said he had seen Sita in Ravana's asoka grove. Her pitiful condition made the monkeys sad. The burning of Lanka made them uproarious with joy. Angada paid a unique compliment to Hanuman: "None is equal to you."

On the way to Kishkindha, the monkeys halted in Madhuvana grove beloved of Sugriva which was guarded zealously. They enjoyed its fruits and ransacked it. The guards, who protected the garden, fled and reported the event to Sugriva, who, hearing about the mad jubilation, concluded that the monkeys had accomplished his command, namely, the discovery of Sita. The monkey horde, summoned back by their king, hurried to Kishkindha.

The momentous mission over, Hanuman conducted himself modestly and properly.

As Angada approached Sugriva, in joy of fulfilment, the latter spoke to Rama: "The godlike Sita has been discovered. There is

no doubt." The clamour of the monkeys filled the hearts of Sugriva, Rama and Lakshmana with joy.

Making respectful obeisance, bowing, Hanuman reported to Rama the discovery of Sita. "She remains constant in her devotion to Rama and is sound in body." His words dropped like nectar. They were precise and were couched in modesty, which earned Rama's appreciation. Beaming with admiration, Rama looked on Hanuman with high regard and compassion. On being asked, Hanuman told Rama every detail of Sita, including her insistence on her rescue within the time-limit set by Ravana. He handed over to Rama the crest jewel which she had entrusted to him.

Rama pressed the jewel to his bosom. Hanuman repeated the words of Sita. He concluded with an affirmation of his assurance to Sita of Rama rescuing her quickly. "Sita, though sorely afflicted with the thought of your excessive grief, derived solace in my presence."

YUDDHA KANDA

The War

Rama was deeply pleased with Hanuman's account of the discovery of Sita. Rama said, "A singular task has been accomplished by you, which could not have been performed by any other hero on earth." It was a momentous mission, which showed his unique qualities. Maruthi was foremost among beings who, when entrusted with a duty, did even more, compatible with that duty.

Rama, throbbing with delight, embraced Hanuman. The idea of the monkeys crossing the sea made Rama thoughtful. He could by virtue of his heroic ability and asceticism dry up the sea for the purpose. He pondered on account of the hordes of monkeys not being able to achieve what Hanuman did.

On being asked, Hanuman gave a detailed and accurate description of Lanka and its fortifications. Thereupon, Rama decided on the strategies.

The monkeys emerged from the caves, mountain tops and trees. They moved along with the generals such as Rishabha, Gandhamadana, Nala, Kumuda, protecting the flanks of the monkey army, with Susena and Jambavan guarding the rear. On Rama's suggestion, Nila led the army along a route rich with fruits, roots, honey and water.

Engaged in Rama's work, the monkeys moved with the velocity of wind, crossing mountains, rivers, lakes. They moved day and night emitting sounds of joy, lashing their tails and stamping their feet, thundering and roaring. They caught sight of the Sahya mountain thick with trees and rich in woodlands. They crossed the mountain, as also the Malaya ranges. The southern sea stretched before them. They rejoiced, seeing the waters lashed by the wind. They saw the sea tossing high with the approach of night, reflecting the images of the moon. The firmament merged with the sea, the waves mingling with the clouds and washing the stars. Full of wonder, the monkeys stood surveying the sea.

Rama, as he stood looking at the sea with the sun sinking, thought of Sita.

In Lanka, Ravana consulted his ministers, army chiefs and generals on the manner of fighting Rama and the monkeys if they crossed the sea. Ministers such as Prahasta vaunted arrogantly, and promised Rama's destruction. Vibhishana advised wisely, "The three worlds know Ravana's splendour. Sita being kept a captive is not a becoming act. The havoc caused in Lanka by Hanuman gives a dire warning of the shape of things to come." He prayed Ravana should renounce anger which destroyed virtues and happiness, and should restore Sita.

The salutary advice had hardly any effect on Ravana. Passion had made Ravana reckless. Dismissing his brother, he retired into his palace. The next day, Vibhishana again advised Ravana. For, the portents following Sita's coming to Lanka were not good. Ravana disdained the advice. He held consultations with his ministers, counsellors, and ignored Vibhishana who presented himself. Ravana issued orders to Prahasta, and his commanders to prepare for the defence of the city.

Hearing it, Vibhishana was in indignation, and warned Sita's abduction and her captivity was unworthy of Ravana, who ignored the distinction between right and wrong. His duty was to neutralize Ravana's unworthy action. Vibhishana, who was dismissed, said: "People who uttered palatable words could be found easily. Seized by death, mighty men have fallen like mounds of sand." He left Lanka.

Coursing through air, Vibhishana reached where Rama stayed. The monkey chiefs, on the ground espied him. Seeing

135

him armed with many weapons, they became suspicious. Gazing on Sugriva and other monkeys, Vibhishana said he was the younger brother of Ravana, who carried off Sita. He had advised his brother to restore Sita to Rama. Impelled by fate, Ravana did not listen to the advice tendered by him. He sought Rama as his refuge.

The monkeys remained cautious and had grave fears. Rama listened to them calmly. Hanuman interceded to say Vibhishana had deliberately come to Rama. Therefore, it seemed advisable to accept him. He argued Vibhishana, on his own judgement, saw superior merit in Rama's cause. His knowledge and counsel would be available to Rama in the encounter with Ravana. He could hardly hide a perfidious motive. His advice would be valuable in storming Lanka.

Hanuman's counsel strengthened Rama's own impression. "I cannot reject one who has come to me in a friendly spirit." Turning to Sugriva, who had a lingering suspicion, he said, "All brothers are not like Bharata; nor are all sons of a father like me; nor are all friends like Sugriva!" Rama vouchsafed security to one who came to him for protection.

Descending on the earth, together with his followers, Vibhishana prostrated at the feet of Rama. He said he came humiliated, he would surrender his sovereignty and even his life to his benefactor who knew right and wrong. Rama looked on Vibhishana with affection and concern.

Vibhishana spoke of Ravana's might. By virtue of a boon from God Brahma, Ravana was incapable of being killed by a god or demon. His brother Kumbhakarna was likewise endowed with incalculable prowess. Prahasta with his strength had defeated the forces of Vaisravana. Indrajit had overpowered Lord Indra. Wearing an invulnerable armour, he was unassailable; he struck the enemy, himself remaining invisible in the battlefield. Ravana's commanders such as Mahodara, Mahaparswa and Akampana were formidable in battle. Ten thousand crores of demons, who were able to change their forms at will, inhabited the city of Lanka.

Rama said: "I know Ravana's feats which stand to his credit. Let him hide or seek refuge in God Brahma himself, he will not escape me. Having killed Ravana, I shall crown you king of Lanka." Vibhishana pledged his assistance to Rama. Lakshmana brought water from the sea and consecrated Vibhishana as the king. The monkeys rejoiced.

Hanuman and Sugriva consulted Vibhishana as to how to cross the sea. Vibhishana thought that the ocean ought to give passage to Lanka. Rama thereupon sat on the sea shore; spreading kusa grass, he lay joining his palms as a gesture of courtesy to sea god, Varuna. For three nights Rama waited for the god to manifest himself. The latter did not. With eyes turned red, Rama told Lakshmana, "Look at the vanity of the ocean. Indeed, calmness and politeness are virtues which could be construed as weakness when directed to those devoid of the virtues." Saying so, Rama loosened a few arrows and sent them into the sea. Flaming, these penetrated deep into the sea water, and raised huge, massive waves. Lakshmana took charge of the bow. Rama warned his arrow would turn the ocean completely dry, and the monkeys could cross to the other shore on foot.

Fitting to his bow the Brahmastra, Rama stood poised to strike. Heaven and earth shook. The sky emitted flashes of lightning. The waters rolled in tempestuous waves, and the tides surged a yojana beyond the shores. Varuna was perturbed. Decked with jewels and gold, and clad in red clothes, the god rose from the sea and, with joined palms, said to Rama: "I shall strive so as to provide a foothold to enable the monkeys to cross over. Let the heroic monkey, Nala, son of the divine architect, Viswakarma, with zeal and love for you, build a sethu (mound) over me. I shall sustain it." So saying, he departed.

Rama directed the leaders of monkeys to have the material collected for Nala to build the bridge. The simian hordes sprang into action on every side. They tore up rocks and trees of all kinds and hurled them into the sea. Hills and mountains were transported. The entire monkey army and its energetic leaders addressed themselves to the arduous task of Rama with joy. The crags, rocks, and the trees stirred up the waters to immense heights. Raising a roar, the monkeys started building the sethu.

The monkeys built fourteen yojanas of the sethu on the first day, twenty yojanas on the second day, twentyone yojanas on the third day, twentytwo yojanas on the fourth day, and twentythree yojanas on the fifth day. The bridge reached up to

the height of mount Suvela, on the opposite side. The work was done in feverish speed. In this way, the bridge, a hundred yojanas wide, was set across the sea, under the guidance of Nala who was gifted with great workmanship, hence Nala-sethu.

The gods, rishis, gandharvas, and other celestials, who appeared in the sky, beheld the marvel. In the poet's words, 'the bright structure across the blue sea cast its charm like the parting of woman's hair'.

Hanuman carried Rama on his back, and Angada carried Lakshmana. The monkeys traversed the sethu, occasionally leaping and darting into the water, and into the air like eagles. The horde camped on the shore in a region with abundance of fruits and fresh water.

Rama felt gratified. The monkeys sallied further into Lanka, watching its unique grandeur. They heard in Lanka the loud clamour of kettle drums, tom-toms. They replied with a roar in a much higher pitch. Organized in formations under the generals, Angada, Nala, Gandhamadana, Jambavan, Susena and others, and protected by Sugriva, Rama and Lakshmana, the monkeys advanced on Lanka. They plucked peaks of mountains, and huge trees as their weapons.

Rama told Sugriva to free Suka, a spy of Ravana whom they had captured. Afflicted by fear, Suka went to Ravana. He reported to him the arrival of Rama, accompanied by the large army of monkeys and bears who crossed the sea. On Ravana's command two of his ministers entered the monkeys' ranks to assess their strength. The spies were captured but Rama, as earlier, let them go. More spies such as Sardula were caught in espionage, and were released through Rama's mercy.

Hearing their submissions, Ravana surveyed from his palace roof Rama's army, which had encamped close to the Suvela mountain. He sought his ministers' counsel.

Ravana took a demon of enormous energy, Vidyujjihva, skilled in conjuring tricks to the asoka grove, where sat Sita. He intended to shake her resolve: "The large army of Rama which swarmed recklessly into Lanka has been annihilated." He laid before Sita, an illusory head, and a mighty bow with an arrow. "Behold the fate of your husband," Ravana said. Sita fell to the ground senseless. Ravana returned to the palace. Regaining consciousness, Sita wailed in agony. Demoness Sarama, who sympathized with Sita, told her she was the victim of an illusion. Rama was alive, and Sita would be rescued. Hearing the mighty din caused by the warlike activities of the monkeys, Sita gained confidence.

Rama accompanied by the monkey chiefs leading their armies

who went forth with the blast of conches and rattle of drums, moved forward.

Ravana commanded his ministers to organize most urgent actions to defend Lanka. Hearing this, Malyavan, his maternal grandfather, reputed for his sagacity, said, 'a monarch, who was adept in the sciences and who trod the path of prudence contended with his enemies as occasion demanded. Yet tact was of much value. For his part, he favoured alliance with Rama to strengthen himself through amiability and friendship.' Ravana rejected the sane advice. He would not surrender Sita. He consulted his ministers, and made arrangements for Lanka's defence. The most powerful leaders of war, including Indrajit, were to guard the four gates of Lanka and its central part.

In the precincts of Lanka, Rama, Sugriva, Hanuman, and other monkeys deliberated. Vibhishana apprised them of the defences built by Ravana, on the basis of reports which his ministers brought to him. Rama detailed the monkeys to storm the gates of Lanka. Rama, along with Lakshmana, Vibhishana, Sugriva and others, stood on the Suvela mountain, and surveyed the city. Lanka lay girt by a wall and packed with warriors who ranged in array looking like an inner defence wall. Beholding the enemies, the exuberant monkeys made clamour of all kinds. Rama stood looking on until night set in and the moon illumined the city. At dawn the commanders of the monkey army entered the parks and gardens on the outskirts of Lanka.

Looking from the summit of Suvela, Rama caught sight of Ravana perched above a gate of his palace. Attired in raiment embroidered with gold, the demon king with his ten heads and twenty arms looked like a massive cloud, enveloped with sunshine.

The incredible happened.

Seized with fury, Sugriva, performing a fantastic feat, sprang on Ravana. Rama, Lakshmana and others looked on, shocked. Grabbing Ravana's marvellous diadem, Sugriva threw it on the ground. A mighty struggle followed between Ravana and Sugriva whose bodies got dyed with blood. Eluding Ravana poised to draw on his supernatural power, Sugriva with a triumphant demeanour sprang into the air. He landed by the side of Rama. The prince, who ever upheld proper conduct, admonished Sugriva for his reckless action which could have brought dire consequences.

The warning was for all. Conduct becoming one's status and dignity would ever be appropriate. Bravado was not heroism. Sugriva's foolishness could have ruined Rama's very mission. His beastly instinct had got better of his kingly position.

Climbing down the mountain, Rama chose a suitable time to march on Lanka. Accordingly the monkey forces went forward in formations and besieged the city. Rama, accompanied by Lakshmana, blocked the northern gate at which Ravana himself had taken up his position. Susena and Jambavan followed by a vast army took up their positions in the rear of Rama. Reaching the eastern gate, Nila, commander-in-chief of the simian forces, took up his position there, with Mainda and Dwivida. Angada, together with Rishabha, Gavaksa, Gaja and other chiefs, occupied the southern gate. Hanuman blocked the western gate. Sugriva placed himself strategically between the northern and western gates. At this position alone, thirty-six crores of monkeys, with their renowned generals, stood exerting pressure on the rakshasas. Lakshmana placed a crore of monkeys at each gate.

The enormous hordes stood expectantly for an encounter. Filled with an inner fury, they lifted up their tails in an unnatural way, bared their teeth and nails to serve as weapons, and their eyes looked suffused with blood, and their faces appeared distorted in wrath. The Trikuta mountain got totally encircled. A crore of monkeys ranged around in surveillance. Lanka stood besieged.

Rama, who observed the strategies of kings, knew the expedients of action, namely, peaceful approach, gift, threat and punishment, sama, dana, bheda and danda. He summoned Angada and asked him to proceed to Ravana, with his message: "The time of retribution has come. Your arrogance has ruined the boon bestowed on you by God Brahma. Having deceived me, meet me in combat. Entering the range of my might, you shall not return alive even if you range all the three worlds."

Ascending in the air, Angada leapt on the palace, where he found Ravana adorned with armlets of gold, holding court. Angada stood before him like a blazing fire. Introducing himself, the emissary delivered Rama's precise message. Fury shook Ravana. He ordered his ministers to put the brash monkey to instant death. Four demons seized the messenger. Angada on his own let himself be held. He rose into the air, with the demons clinging to him. They fell to the ground. Thereafter, Angada leapt on the top of Ravana's palace, which he violently cleft asunder; Ravana stood gazing. Shouting his name, Angada rose into the air, and returned to Rama. Ravana was astounded to witness the feat of the son of Bali.

The rakshasa army, mobilized by Ravana, went into action. They beat their drums and emitted a terrible roar. The war began. The monkeys raised their cry: "Victory to king Sugriva!" This was matched by the rakshasas who shouted: "Victory to Ravana!"

The rakshasas attacked the enemies with flaming maces, javelins, pikes and axes. The monkeys answered with uprooted trees and torn mountain tops. Their tails, nails and teeth did havoc. Monkeys of gigantic proportions went into action. The hordes in explosive fury confronted the adversaries who were mounted on elephants and on chariots. Many duels took place.

Indrajit contended with Angada, and Prajangha with Sampathi. Virupaksha grappled with Lakshmana. Indrajit struck Angada with his mace, who in turn attacked the enemy's shining chariot and horses.

Sugriva caused havoc. The mighty Gaja fought the ogre Tapana. Vibhishana and the valorous Lakshmana coordinated closely on the battlefield. Hanuman grappled with many ferocious giants himself.

Sugriva killed Praghasa, who was plaguing the monkey army. Virupaksha of fearful aspect was assailed by a hail of shafts from Lakshmana. Four rakshasas, Agniketu, Rashmiketu, Suptaghna and Yajnakopa attacked Rama. His arrows killed all.

Nikumbha pierced Nila with his pointed arrows. Pulling out a chariot wheel, Nila hit both the demon and his charioteer and killed them. The indomitable ogre, Pratapana, fell at the hands of Nala of great vehemence. The heroic Susena in a contest with Vidyunmali, hurled a huge rock and crushed the demon's chest.

In this way, innumerable duels took place between the rakshasas and the energetic monkeys puffed with fury. The battlefield was littered with broken maces, javelins, lances, arrows, shattered chariots, slain horses, elephants, and headless trunks. The scene was ghastly. With darkness setting in on sunset, the strength of the demons doubled, to assail the monkeys from all sides. So tortured, the monkeys in fury sprang up in the air and tore with their sharp teeth the chariots, their horses, golden ornaments, and pennants. The monkeys dragged the elephants.

With their shafts darting like snakes, Rama and Lakshmana killed a multitude of demons. Pulverised by the hooves of horses, the elephants' legs, and the wheels of the chariots, dust enveloped the battlefield that smelt strongly of blood flowing in streams. The sounds of kettle drums, wooden tom-toms and drums, with the blasts of conches, rattling of wheels raised a tumult. In the dreadful darkness, the demons assailed Rama himself. Rama's arrows leaping like tongues of flame struck them down. They included mighty demons Yagnasatru, Mahaparswa, Mahodara, Vajradamshtra, Suka and Sarana. Some, though pierced, slipped away even as Rama's flaming arrows lit up the quarters. The night looked autumnal as if illumined by fireflies.

Amidst the din, the gigantic golangulas (monkeys, who were long-tailed and black-faced, dark as night) crushed the demons to death. The heroic Angada struck Indrajit and his charioteer and horses. The latter killed, Indrajit fled. The rishis and gods, who witnessed the combat from above, as also Rama and Lakshmana, applauded Angada's doing. The monkeys cried out 'well done'!

In a terrible rage, Indrajit while remaining invisible, loosed shafts bright as lightning. He confounded Rama and Lakshmana, and fighting treacherously he assailed the brothers with arrows that worked as venomous snakes.

Baffled by the conjuring trick, Rama employed ten mighty monkey generals including Nila, Angada, Sarabha, Dwivida, Hanuman, Sanuprastha, Rishabha and Rishabhaskandha to find out the whereabouts of Indrajit. However, Indrajit remaining hidden plagued the monkeys and Rama and Lakshmana with magical shafts. He roared. Pierced in their limbs and covered with the heads of arrows, the princes staggered and fell to the ground. Rama and Lakshmana bound lay motionless on bed of arrows. The monkeys were gripped by desperation. Indrajit remaining veiled by his occult power rejoiced, "The exploits of Rama and Lakshmana and of the monkeys were rendered void

145

like the clouds in autumn." Indrajit boasted, roared and laughed. The demons thundered.

The princes lay motionless as if devoid of life. Indrajit entered the city in triumph.

Vibhishana said to Sugriva, whose face was bathed in tears, that Rama and Lakshmana would shake off their swoon.

The foremost among the monkeys including Hanuman, Angada, Nila, Susena, Jambavan guarded Rama and Lakshmana. They remained alert.

Ravana was full of pride over Indrajit's victory. On his orders the demons and demonesses, who guarded Sita, put her, along with Trijata, in Pushpaka. The aerial chariot flew over the city. Looking down, Sita saw the demons in jubilant mood, and the monkeys with agony standing by the side of Rama and Lakshmana who had fallen. Seized with sorrow, Sita burst into tears. Trijata consoled her, "Rama and Lakshmana could not have been killed," and took her back to the asoka grove. Rama gained consciousness. Lakshmana continued to lie bound, and bathed in blood. He was in deep anguish.

On request by Sugriva, Jambavan restored the confidence of the monkeys.

Meanwhile, there arose a wind, as also clouds with flashes of lightning. All heard a flutter of wings. It shook the Trikuta mountain, and large trees fell headlong into the sea. The serpents in the island got alarmed. In an instant, the monkeys saw Garuda descending from the sky like a blazing fire. The serpents, which had bound Rama and Lakshmana, fled in mortal fear. Touching Rama and Lakshmana, the mighty eagle wiped their bodies. Their wounds got cicatrized and their bodies turned bright and smooth. Their strength and radiance got redoubled. Garuda embraced them. Rama praised Garuda. Wishing the Lord victory, Garuda took leave, soaring in

the sky. The monkey hordes raised a victorious clamour.

The demons reported to Ravana the recovery of Rama and Lakshmana. Ravana, who got much perturbed, ordered the mobilization of his entire forces for war.

In the battles that followed, Hanuman killed Dhrumraksa, a leader of demons. Ravana thereupon despatched Vajradamshtra, whom Angada killed. Many ferocious demons issued forth to fight monkeys. Among these, Akampana was annihilated by Hanuman. Prahasta, who sallied forth with a huge army, was killed by Nila. Thereupon, the army of the demons fell back.

Hearing the many disasters, particularly the death of Prahasta, Ravana, who shook with anger, decided to proceed to the battlefield to destroy the enemies. Wearing his golden diadem, over which shone a canopy radiant as the moon, he ascended a chariot which was yoked to a team of the foremost horses. Sounds of conches and beating of kettle drums, loud clapping of arms and menacing roars filled the air. His ten pairs of eyes blazed. He saw the army of the monkeys spread like a wild forest, brandishing trees and rocks, and roaring wildly. He was accompanied by the illustrious Trisira and many army commanders.

Ravana began splitting asunder the sea of monkeys with his arrows. Seeing him advance menacingly, Sugriva darted forth hurling a mountain top at the demon king. Ravana tore it asunder with arrows with golden shafts. In rage he loosed an arrow resembling a huge serpent for the destruction of Sugriva. Hit by the shaft, Sugriva fell and fainted. Several monkey chiefs including Nala rushed to the spot; struck by the streams of arrows, they too fell to the ground. The monkeys sought Rama for protection. Seizing his bow, Rama went forth. Lakshmana joined him.

Ravana covered the monkeys with torrents of arrows. Seeing

the assault, Hanuman darted towards Ravana with his right hand raised. "Call to your mind the fate of your son, Aksha," he roared. Taunted so, Ravana hit Hanuman on the chest, who reeled like a top. Steadying, the son of wind god struck Ravana with his steely palms. Ravana shook a la a mountain in an earthquake. A shout of joy was heard from the sky.

Recovering, Ravana turned to Nila, who hoisted a mountain top and hurled it. Seven arrows struck it down. Reducing his huge form to a diminutive size, Nila jumped on to the top of Ravana's standard, and then to his diadem. Ravana was wonder-struck at the agility and energy of the monkey. Recovering from his confusion, Ravana invoked the missile presided over by fire god, and loosed it. Hit in the chest by the blazing arrow, Nila toppled.

Turning to Lakshmana, Ravana let fly seven arrows which Soumitri tore to pieces. A divine javelin, which shone like fire, pierced Lakshmana's chest. The prince, who got grievously hurt, fell unconscious. Ravana, leaping to the ground, tried to lift Lakshmana with his twenty arms, which had lifted Kailasa mountain, yet he could not raise Soumitri! While engaged in the effort, he was struck in the chest by Hanuman's powerful feet. Under its impact, the lord of demons fell on his knees in the chariot and lay prostrate. Blood flowed from his mouths, eyes and ears. He was dazed.

Hanuman prayed to Rama: "Do climb on my shoulders, as God Vishnu on Garuda, and destroy Ravana." Sitting on Hanuman's back, Rama faced Ravana in his chariot. His bowstring caused a sound like the clap of thunder. He spoke to Ravana: "If you fly to Indra, Yama (Lord of death), Brahma, or Siva, for refuge, you shall not escape my wrath." Advancing, Rama tore Ravana's armour to pieces, and destroyed his steeds, chariot wheels, standard, canopy, pennon, and the charioteer.

He struck Ravana, who let fall his bow. Seeing him swooning, Rama using an arrow with a crescent-shaped head tore Ravana's diadem. In a true spirit of gallantry, Rama said, "I shall not put you to death straightaway. Depart, come forth again mounted on a chariot. You shall witness my strength."

Ravana withdrew.

Witness Rama's conduct which was full of confidence and nobility! He did not take advantage of Ravana's plight. He would wait for a proper fight. On the other hand, see its effect on Ravana. His vanity was bruised! His mind was, for the first time, troubled.

Ravana sat on his throne and reflected. He was defeated by a mere mortal! The words of God Brahma were coming true. He remained vulnerable to danger from a human being as against immunity from death at the hands of gods, celestials, demons, yakshas, serpents! He imagined Sita was Vedavati (an apsara) whom he had sought to offend. The curse of Parvathi, Nandikeswara, the celestial nymphs, such as Rambha and Punjikasthala, were coming true!

Ravana ordered that his brother Kumbhakarna, with immeasurable strength, be roused from sleep.

The henchmen of Ravana proceeded to Kumbhakarna's abode, taking with them perfumery, garlands, and an immense quantity of food. It was subterranean, one yojana wide on every side. The attendants placed before him a heap of food for his gratification—antelopes, buffaloes and plenty of victuals, pails of liquid. They daubed him with sandal-paste, and sweet perfumes. They burnt incense. They set up a great clamour to awaken him. Horses, donkeys, camels and elephants, which were whipped up, trod on him. The entire Lanka was filled with the noise of the effort, yet Kumbhakarna did not wake up. The attendants poured hundreds of pails of water into his ears.

Mallets studded with nails struck him, on head, chest and limbs. Tops of trees struck heavy blows on him.

Thus interrupted in his sleep, Kumbhakarna felt being tormented by hunger. Stretching his limbs from drowsiness, Kumbhakarna sprang to his feet all at once. He consumed the victuals of various kinds and drank fat and wines.

His hunger and thirst having been satisfied, Kumbhakarna enquired if everything was well with the king. He would not have awakened him for a trivial reason.

The demons narrated what had happened, in the wake of the abduction of Sita—the death of prince Aksha, the burning of Lanka, the siege of Lanka, the war. Kumbhakarna shook

the earth with his strides as he hastened to Ravana. Seeing Kumbhakarna, the monkeys got alarmed. Many fell down; some sought Rama; many seized with panic fled in all directions. With his diadem, Kumbhakarna walked sky-high. Vibhishana narrated to Rama the story of Kumbhakarna.

As Kumbhakarna met Ravana, the latter hailed him and asked him to destroy Rama's army.

Kumbhakarna, while amenable, was not devoid of moral sense. He said disaster had come to Ravana as Vibhishana and he had feared. The result of Ravana's deed of bringing away Sita came speedily. In the pride of his prowess he did not distinguish between right and wrong. Men who tendered

unwholesome advice should be excluded from counsel to the king.
On the contrary, the advice uttered by Mandodari, his beloved
consort, and by Vibhishana was salutary. Ravana spurned it.

Ravana in rage said that the brave did not grieve over the
bygone. Kumbhakarna should nullify the consequences that
flowed from his deed. Kumbhakarna said that even as he gave
Ravana salutary advice, he would do what was fit out of affection
for his brother. He warned that even the wise, who persisted in
folly in the conceit of their strength, fell. Those who joined causes
without their hearts in them would lose. Thereafter, the giant,
taking an imposing bow, sallied forth to join the battle.

Kumbhakarna moved forward propelled as he was by destiny.
Armed with an iron club, besides other weapons, Kumbhakarna
looked like the god of destruction (Kalarudra) at the end of the
world cycle. The monkeys stampeded. The generals decided to
fight the enormous giant. Fallen on the demon, rocks and trees

154

with blossoms, split. In the panic, some monkeys leapt into
the sea and drowned. "Fleeing will end our glory," Angada
warned. Regaining courage, the generals, including Dwivida
and Hanuman, marched ahead leading the simian forces.

Kumbhakarna thundered. The monkeys hit him with mountain tops and trees. He destroyed the monkeys as a fire would consume a forest. A devastating struggle followed. Struck by the giant, several thousand monkeys lay scattered on the ground. Folding in his arms several monkeys in a single effort, he started devouring them. Traversing in air, Hanuman carried peaks, rocks and trees of every kind and attacked the giant. He hit the demon with a mace, and the blow bathed the enemy in blood. Brandishing a spike, Kumbhakarna assailed Hanuman on the breast. That threw the latter out of his wits, and the rakshasas highly rejoiced at the hero's discomfiture. Mighty monkeys Rishabha, Sarabha, Mainda, Dhumra, Susena, Nila, Kumuda, Gavaksa, and many others attacked Kumbhakarna with crags, trees, their hands, feet, fists. The monkeys in thousands climbed on the enemy, into his mouth, and issued forth through his nostrils, and ears.

Angada, who was attacked, slapped the enemy with vehemence on his chest. Under the impact, the demon fainted. Regaining consciousness, he struck Angada. The monkey prince fell.

Kumbhakarna rushed to Sugriva. The heroes were matched. An extraordinary encounter followed. Kumbhakarna struck Sugriva with the peak of a mountain. The king of monkeys fell senseless. Lifting him, Kumbhakarna bore Sugriva away! Seized by shock, the monkeys scattered.

The son of wind god said to himself: 'We would do what was fit to do. He for his part could kill the ogre. That would be inappropriate. For the king of monkeys would gain his freedom himself. If any others freed him, it would blemish the king's reputation! The odium of having been saved by a subject of his would remain on his mind.'

One cannot help admiring Hanuman's sagacity. He was ever an adept in appropriate action.

As Kumbhakarna entered Lanka carrying Sugriva, the demons lined the roads, and stood on terraces, showering flowers and pouring down scented water. As the irony would have it, the very fragrance, and the coolness of the royal highway helped Sugriva to revive. He pondered. He acted in a characteristic manner. All of a sudden, he tore off with his mighty nails the ears of Kumbhakarna, bit off his nose, and split open his sides with his huge toes. Frenzied in pain and wrath, Kumbhakarna thrashed the monkey king against the ground. So freed, Sugriva bounced into the air, and landed in the presence of Rama! He was drenched in blood.

Kumbhakarna re-emerged, more determined. He devoured monkeys, gathering them with his arms, even a hundred at a time. Lakshmana covered the demon with his arrows.

Kumbhakarna said vainly, "I, for my part, do seek Rama." Unruffled, Lakshmana pointed to his brother, who stood nearby. The rakshasa rushed past Lakshmana towards Rama.

Rama dug arrows with mystic potency in the chest of Kumbhakarna. Stung, the demon darted forward in full fury. The arrows deprived him of all his weapons, which lay scattered in the battlefield. Unarmed, with streams of blood flowing down his massive form, Kumbhakarna ran about devouring the monkeys, bears and all. Seizing a mountain peak, the ogre hurled it at Rama. With seven shafts, Rama split it in the air. Harassed hard, Kumbhakarna fell, and while falling he knocked down hundreds of monkeys. The monkeys from all sides climbed over him. The demon shook them off. Rama wielding his tremendous bow darted towards the giant, "Know me to be your destroyer." Kumbhakarna laughed hideously: "I should not be taken for Viradha or Kabandha or Khara or Maricha or Bali himself," he boasted.

Kumbhakarna brandished a mace, and wrought immense destruction around. Thereupon, Rama struck him with a mystic missile presided over by wind god, which cut the arm that wielded the mace. Torn of one arm, the giant raised an alarming cry. Rama slashed his uplifted arm that held trees to strike. Arms severed, the giant rushed on violently. Two crescent-shaped arrows from Rama severed his feet. The sea and the earth resounded with the thud of the falling limbs. Thereafter, Rama charged an arrow with a missile presided over by Indra, and discharged it. Brilliant as fire, the shaft fled and tore off the giant's head. The fabulous head, as it fell, demolished mansions, gates and a part of the city's defence wall. Kumbhakarna's body borne by the missile crashed into the sea.

The gods raised a loud shout of joy. The celestials, sages, rishis, yakshas and gandharvas rejoiced witnessing the prowess of Rama. The monkeys danced in delirious joy.

On hearing the death of Kumbhakarna, Ravana fainted. Recovering, he lamented, "My right hand is gone! This is the fruit of my action in expelling Vibhishana."

Ravana's sons and brothers joined the fight. Narantaka was killed by Angada, and Devantaka and Trisira by Hanuman. The brothers, Mahodara was killed by Nila, and Mahaparswa by Rishaba.

Atikaya, on whom God Brahma had bestowed a boon of invincibility, struck terror in the monkeys.

Vibhishana acquainted Rama with the might of Atikaya, son of Ravana through his consort Dhanyamalini. He acquired many boons from the Creator such as immunity from death at the hands of gods and demons, his heavenly armour and the bright chariot. The monkeys rushed to him. Atikaya massacred the monkeys wholesale fighting like a 'furious lion puffed with the pride of youth, striking terror in a flock of deer'.

A terrible fight ensued between Atikaya and Soumitri. The Vidyadharas, gods, demons and rishis, yakshas arrived to witness the duel. It was a well-matched encounter, which reached a grim deadlock. Seeing this, wind god whispered into Lakshmana's ears: "The demon is clad in an impenetrable armour, he should be pierced with a missile presided over by God Brahma." As Soumitri fitted the missile to his bow, the vault of heaven shook and the earth cracked. The shaft he flung flew with the speed of Garuda. It defied all weapons employed by the giant. The missile raging like fire severed the head of Atikaya. With his diadem he precipitately fell on the ground. The monkeys paid homage to the valour of Lakshmana. The latter sought the presence of Rama.

Ravana became disconsolate. He enjoined on the generals to adopt very special strategies to defend the city, especially the asoka grove where Sita sat. The redoubtable Indrajit submitted: "Behold Rama lying dead along with Lakshmana on the earth today. The gods, the sun and the moon shall witness my unchallenged prowess." So bragging, Meghanada ascended a chariot, swift as the wind, and equipped with fierce implements of war. True to his heroic nature and dauntless bravery, he zealously sought the battlefield.

Exhibiting much vehemence, many powerful and egregious demons accompanied him, riding elephants, horses, tigers and other mounts. They carried lances, spears, swords, axes, maces, bhusundis (firearms), mallets, parighas (bludgeons studded with iron). Blasts of conches and kettle drums shocked the air. The prince decked with dazzling ornaments and riding in his magnificent chariot, the vanquisher of Lord Indra, indeed made an impressive procession. Ravana blessed his son: "No warrior could be your rival, not even among the gods, not to speak of a mortal man, Rama."

Reaching the battlefield, Indrajit worshipped fire god, with spells of great potency. He invoked the missile presided over by God Brahma and charged the bow with the invocatory spell. As he did it to the accompaniment of oblations to fire, the vault of heaven shook. The famed warrior was aflame with lustre.

Indrajit, as was his wont, hid himself from view in the sky. From there he did his massacre, tearing the monkey army with volleys of arrows. Agonized and distracted, the monkeys stampeded. The trees, rocks and mountain peaks which they threw up surrounded Indrajit even as he remained concealed and unhurt. He pierced Gandhamadana with eighteen arrows, Nala with nine arrows, Malinda with seven arrows, and Gaja with five arrows, Jambavan with ten arrows, and Nila with thirty arrows. Striking with mystic missiles he rendered lifeless, as it were, Sugriva, as well as Rishabha, Angada and Dwivida. Rama's army came under a hail of shafts and missiles, spikes, swords, maces, clubs, nalikas (broad-headed arrows) and axes shooting up incandescent flames and sparks. The monkey forces, bathed in blood, their bodies mutilated, ran helter-skelter.

As the war raged, Indrajit's energy grew like a swollen fire. He attacked from all directions. Remaining invisible, he let fall arrows even as a dark cloud would pour masses of water. His conjuring tricks dazed the monkeys. Bleeding profusely, the monkeys, said the poet, looked like huge trees bearing crimson flowers. Looking up to the sky, they got struck in their eyes. Employing weapons with magical powers, Indrajit pierced the monkey chiefs including Hanuman, Sugriva, Angada, Jambavan and Nila.

Having wounded the leaders of the monkeys, Meghanada showered shining shafts on Rama and Lakshmana. The Brahmastra, which he used, struck Rama and Lakshmana. They fell. Indrajit shouted in joy. Having prostrated the princes, as also the monkey army, he withdrew all at once. He narrated his exploits to Ravana, who was thrilled by his son's feat!

As Rama and Lakshmana lay senseless, Sugriva and the monkey commanders, Nila, Angada, and Jambavan felt nonplussed. Seeing the despondency, Vibhishana said, "Respecting the missile presided over by God Brahma, the princes let themselves be overwhelmed."

Thereafter, Vibhishana and Hanuman with torches ranged the battlefield as an army of many crores of monkeys lay senseless under the spell employed by Indrajit. They searched for Jambavan, hallowed in age and wisdom. Approaching him, Vibhishana addressed him, "We hope, sir, that your life is not put out." Jambavan said, "Your voice makes me recognize you, for I hardly see you with my eyes." He asked, "Does Hanuman live? He is not only blessed but made his parents blessed." Vibhishana queried, "You have not enquired of Rama and Lakshmana, of Sugriva, of Angada!"

Jambavan said, "For, if the hero among the heroes breathes, our army lives."

Going close to Jambavan and clasping his feet, Anjaneya saluted him, with humility. Hearing the words, the bear responded, "You are consummate in valour and power, you can save the monkeys, and heal Rama and Lakshmana. None other. You should leap to the Himalaya mountain, which has two splendid peaks. These are the Rishabha in golden lustre and the Kailasa shining like silver. These are laid with medicinal herbs of rare power. These include the four luminous herbs which have great potency, mritasanjivani (to bring life to the dead); visalyakarani (to extract weapons and heal wounds); suvarnakarani (to restore the body to the original complexion); and sandhani (to join severed limbs). Collecting the four herbs, O, son of wind god, you ought to come back with utmost speed."

The administration filled Hanuman with incalculable power. He remembered who he was. With the force of wind he grew

into a measureless form. Trodden by him, the Trikuta mountain swayed. Peaks got shattered. Stricken with panic the city of Lanka shook. Maruthi sprang to the Malaya mountain thickly set with springs and trees. Pressing the mountain fully with his feet, and opening his mouth which shone like a fire, he let out a roar that made the demons shudder. Bowing to sea god, the servant of Rama raised his enormous tail, and leapt into the air. Stretching his arms, Hanuman made for the Himalaya mountain.

He seemed engaged, childlike, in a wager with his father, wind god, as he coursed through the heaven! The celestials rejoiced.

Reaching the Himalayan peaks bearing the divine herbs, Hanuman ranged searching for them. He failed to identify them. This filled his heart with dismay and wrath, his eyes glowing fiercely. Impelled by the urgency, Hanuman vehemently severed the mountain tops that bore the herbs, and carrying the crags in his hands, sped away. The gods gazed at the extraordinary event and all creation throbbed with joy. Hanuman, who was impelled by his love for Rama, landed on the Trikuta mountain. The monkeys emitted a frightful roar. Greeting the monkey chiefs, with his countenance glowing in joy, Maruthi embraced Vibhishana.

Inhaling the unique life-giving fragrance of the herbs, wafted in the kindly wind, Rama and Lakshmana revived. The entire army was healed of the wounds and restored, and they sprang on their feet as a vast forest humbled by the mighty wind rising from the ground. The herbs made them feel awake as from a sleep!

Hanuman carried the crags bearing the herbs and deposited them in the Himalaya. Returning with the speed of thought, he joined Rama.

It was evening. Under the orders of Sugriva, the monkeys set fire to the towering gates of Lanka, attics, streets and byways. The wind raged in immense joy. Mansions toppled, aloe, sandalwood trees and precious material such as silk, gems burnt. Palaces fell, ornaments of horses, elephants, chariots, swords, bows, lances, and all kinds of weapons burnt. Archways were enveloped in fire. Women screamed.

Feeling invigorated, Rama and Lakshmana seized their bows and arrows. Rama let go a twang which struck terror in the hearts of the enemies. Assailed by his shafts, the principal gates of Lanka crumbled to the ground.

The demons, on orders of Ravana, emerged in full force. Kumbha and Nikumbha, sons of Kumbhakarna, joined the battle. Sugriva for his part ordered the monkeys to mount an intense assault. The battle presented a phenomenal spectacle in the moonlight.

In the struggle that followed fierce demons fell. Death came to Kampana at the hands of Angada, and to Kumbha at the hands of Sugriva, amongst many other giants. Nikumbha seized a club that resembled a mountain crag, plated with gold and decked with diamonds and corals, and roaring with his mouth wide open, he stood frightening the demons and the monkeys. Neither dared to move. Even so, baring his bosom, Hanuman stood in front. With vigour he pounded the demon's chest. The latter's armour cracked, blood shooting forth in many streams. Nikumbha staggered; yet he grappled with Hanuman, and carried him off. Striking the demon with his fists, Hanuman, supremely agile, disengaged himself, threw Nikumbha down, and tore his head. Seeing the feat, the simian army roared in excessive joy.

Hearing the news, Ravana flared up, and commanded Makaraksha, son of Khara, to make short work of Rama and Lakshmana. The rakshasa drove in full speed, boasting loudly. Rejoiced at his braggadocio, the demons ran along, amidst the tumult of thousands of conches and kettle drums, leonine roars and clapping of hands. The monkeys fled. Rama interposed; the demon vowed he would avenge the death of his father who was killed by Rama in the Dandaka forest. Rama split the enemy's chariot, and struck him down by a mystic missile presided over by fire god.

Possessed with violent anger on the death of Makaraksha, Ravana summoned Indrajit. Having poured oblations into the sacred fire to gratify the gods, Indrajit ascended a splendid chariot, drawn by four horses, which had the magical power of becoming invisible. Looking forbidding, he bragged: "Having rid the earth of monkeys and of Rama and Lakshmana, I shall bring supreme joy to my father."

He rushed into the fray.

Remaining out of sight, Indrajit enveloped the princes with whetted arrows. As Rama and Lakshmana covered the sky with arrows, Indrajit by dint of conjuring tricks, plunged the quarters in darkness. Pierced deeply by golden shafts, the brothers appeared like two kadamba trees in blossom. The monkeys fell on the earth in hundreds. Lakshmana, who would fain use the Brahmastra for the total destruction of Indrajit and his forces, was admonished by Rama: "You ought not to kill one who lies hidden, or is fleeing. We shall endeavour to destroy Indrajit alone."

Divining the intention of Rama, Indrajit re-entered the scene. Resorting to deception, he kept an illusory Sita in his chariot, and advanced menacingly. Facing the monkey horde and unsheathing his sword, he held Sita by her hair, who cried 'Rama, O, Rama.' The sight filled Hanuman with agony. He addressed Indrajit, "Woe for your sinful conduct." Along with other monkeys he rushed in vehemence towards the demon. Indrajit said, "I am going to make short work of Sita; while you stand looking on, I shall then kill the princes, Sugriva, the unworthy Vibhishana and yourself." Sliced by a sharp-edged sword, Sita fell on the ground. Gripped in melancholy, the monkeys sped.

Indrajit proceeded to the sanctuary, called Nikumbhila, poured oblations into the sacred fire. Hearing Sita was done to death, Rama swooned. On being told by Vibhishana of Indrajit's confusing trick, Rama revived. Vibhishana warned that if Indrajit was permitted to complete the oblations, he would become invincible. The ritual should be prevented. "When he is killed, Ravana is killed."

Lakshmana with a huge army proceeded to Nikumbhila. He was accompanied by Vibhishana. Wielding one of the foremost of bows and touching his brother's feet, he said, "My arrows will destroy Indrajit this very day." He walked round Rama in reverence. Accompanied by Hanuman and Angada, Lakshmana dented the enemy army. The demons counter-attacked. The confrontation was a tumultuous one. Hearing his army being harassed and dispirited, Indrajit, proud as ever, got up even as the ritual remained incomplete. He mounted his chariot which was kept ready. Then followed between the monkeys and the demons one of the most spectacular encounters. With his coppery face and red eyes, and armed with a massive bow, Indrajit looked like death itself. The ogres ranged around him. Hanuman battered them with uprooted trees and wrought havoc. Thousands of demons covered Hanuman with a hail of weapons. He was struck on all sides. Seeing Hanuman, Indrajit drove to that spot. Hanuman challenged him: "Withstand my power, then you will be accounted as one of the foremost heroes."

Vibhishana pointed out Indrajit to Lakshmana and asked him to kill him without permitting him to complete his oblations. Lakshmana gazed on the infamous hero of immense might. He challenged Indrajit to a straight encounter.

On seeing Vibhishana in proximity, Indrajit addressed him, "How do you bear hostility to me, your son? You are pitiable. Even if a stranger is endowed with all excellences, and one's own kinsman is devoid of these, the latter is preferable to one who has no sense of honour."

Vibhishana replied, "How can your father expel his own brother? The wise disapprove one who is intent on his own destruction. Neither my brother nor you, caught in the noose of death, will survive. You spoke harshly to me. When you come within range of Lakshmana's weapons, however much you display your celebrated might, you will not return alive today."

Filled with anger on hearing the pronouncement, Indrajit lifted a powerful bow, ascended a huge chariot drawn by black horses, and equipped it with all weapons. He beheld Lakshmana mounted on the back of Hanuman. He said, "The shafts from my bow will consume your body as fire consumes a pile of cotton. Earlier your brother and you were laid low by me. Today, facing me, you are on your way to the lord of death." Lakshmana decried the boast: "Remaining invisible in the battlefield is the method of thieves, not of heroes. It is inglorious to brag." Showering whetted arms, Indrajit said he would destroy Lakshmana, who in turn replied: "I shall kill you without offering a harsh remark or reviling you."

Lakshmana dug into Indrajit's breast five arrows, with the bow-string drawn to his ear. Indrajit pranced the enemy in return. They fought like two lions. Finding Lakshmana indefatigable, Indrajit's face started becoming pale. Vibhishana noticed it, and asked Lakshmana to take advantage of the adversary's mood of despair. Assailed fiercely, Indrajit stood stupefied for a while. Recovering, with his eyes turned to Lakshmana and seeing him immovable, he pierced Lakshmana with seven arrows, and Hanuman with ten shafts. In fury, he pierced Vibhishana too, with a hundred arrows. Thereupon Lakshmana mounted a most intensive assault on Indrajit. The latter's golden armour fell in pieces in the chariot like a maze of stars. He was wounded. Indignant beyond measure, Indrajit pierced Lakshmana with a thousand arrows. The two fought with their limbs lacerated. They were bathed all over in blood. Their arrows flew, clashed and fell like a heavy rain from the destructive clouds amidst a dreadful clamour.

Vibhishana guided the monkey chiefs to destroy totally Indrajit's army, which remained heavily pressed. Jambavan took the lead.

The battle between the heroes went on with victory for neither. The sun sank, and the battlefield got dark.

Resuming the battle, Lakshmana pierced the steeds yoked to Indrajit's chariot. Then using a gilded arrow, shot with full force, he severed the head of the charioteer. Thereupon, Indrajit himself played the role of the charioteer. Lakshmana sent forth streams of shafts. Charioteer gone, and fully exposed in the battlefield, Indrajit lost zest for the combat. He grew despondent. Rejoiced, the monkeys of rare might fell on the horses of Indrajit which, crushed and mutilated, sank lifeless on the ground. Indrajit leapt down from the chariot. He withdrew into the city.

Mounting another chariot, and with a charioteer who could read the minds of the horses, Indrajit sallied forth, surrounded by select battalions, impelled by the force of destiny. So accompanied, Meghanada assaulted Lakshmana and also Vibhishana.

Five arrows from Lakshmana pierced the enemy's bosom and, going through his body, fell to the ground. His bow was split. Indrajit took a stronger one with a stout cord, and let loose powerful arrows on Lakshmana, who successfully intercepted them. With an arrow known as bhalla, he cut off the head of Indrajit's charioteer. The horses continued to draw the chariot— a rare sight! Lakshmana struck them with arrows which threw them into panic. Extremely indignant, Indrajit poured a volley of arrows and hurt Lakshmana in the forehead. Lakshmana, in turn, hit Indrajit in his face. Smeared all over with blood, the two heroes fought on. Indrajit also attacked Vibhishana, who in turn struck down with his mace the horses of his nephew. Leaping down from the chariot, Indrajit hurled his javelin on his uncle, and Lakshmana split it into pieces.

Lakshmana and Indrajit proved equal to each other. They exchanged many divine missiles. All created beings gazed in wonder.

Lakshmana trained an arrow, presided over by Lord Indra, and drawing the bowstring full, uttered the prayer: "If Rama, son of Dasaratha, has set his mind on virtue and is true to his promise and is unrivalled in prowess, let the son of Ravana be destroyed." He flung the missile. It flew straight to its target, severed the head of Indrajit adorned with flaming earrings, casque and all, from his trunk. The hero's head fell on the earth's surface.

The monkey forces were in intense jubilation. They harried the rakshasa army which ran stupefied. Many fled deep into Lanka, many plunged into the sea. The poet says, even as sunbeams tarry no longer when the sun has gone below the horizon, the demons vanished in all directions. The gods in heaven beat the drums, the nymphs danced, and the gandharvas sang. The sky rained flowers.

Vibhishana, Sugriva, Jambavan, Hanuman, and other monkey chiefs heartily applauded Lakshmana. Leaning on Vibhishana and Hanuman, Lakshmana went to Rama, and respectfully stood beside him. Vibhishana reported the ghastly end of Indrajit. Rama experienced unusual joy, "Well done, O, Lakshmana, a great feat indeed!" said Rama who drew his abashed brother into his lap and embraced him. He told Susena that Lakshmana's wounds from weapons be healed quickly.

The ministers reported to Ravana the death of Indrajit at the hands of Lakshmana, assisted by Vibhishana. Ravana swooned. Recovering after a long time, he fell a prey to grief as never before. He was overwhelmed by anger, flames bursting forth from his mouths.

Ravana decided on the destruction of Sita.

Armed with a sword, and accompanied by Mandodari and by his ministers, Ravana entered the asoka grove, roaring wildly. Sita was scared. 'I am sure to be destroyed today,' she thought. Seeing her wailing, a minister, Suparaswa cautioned, 'how could we kill a woman, who is in our care? Rather we should, if we can, annihilate Rama!' The abductor withdrew.

Ravana sat in the assembly, ferocious like a wounded lion.

He ordered that accompanied by the entire army of elephants, horses, chariots and foot-soldiers, the commanders should go to the battlefield. He would destroy Rama.

Towards sunrise a multitude of rakshasa formations went into action with all available weapons. The monkey hordes for their part armed themselves heavily with rocks, trees, maces, and other weapons. As the contending forces clashed, clouds of dust rose, and blood flowed in streams, carrying the corpses of elephants, horses, chariots, and demons. The monkeys tore off with their teeth and nails the hairs, ears, brows, noses of the ogres. A hundred monkey leaders rushed at each single enemy on the battlefield.

Rama, penetrating deep into the enemy ranks, and moving like lightning, performed deeds never witnessed before. The demons could not discover Rama any more than 'one could see a blast blowing in a forest!' The poet said, 'the enemy forces could not see Rama any more than created beings were able to perceive their souls.' The demons exclaimed, 'there was Rama exterminating the elephants; there was Rama destroying the car-warriors; there was Rama killing foot-soldiers along with the horses.' Rama was everywhere; confused, the rakshasas slew one another in rage. At times they saw thousands of Ramas in the battlefield, at times one. They saw the golden ends of his bow revolving like a firebrand, and the havoc it wrought but not Rama himself! He appeared like a flaming discus burning the enemies. The battlefield resembled the ground where God Rudra disported himself after destruction of the evil ones. The celestials applauded Rama's achievement in a part of a day! Rama stood unwearied in action.

Brimming with bravado, laughing hoarsely, Ravana said that with the arrows loosed from his bow he would despatch Rama and Lakshmana on that day to the abode of Yama. He would avenge the death of Khara, Kumbhakarna, Prahasta and Indrajit. He would slay the monkeys, who lying dead would carpet the earth. The commanders proclaimed the message loudly everywhere. More than a lakh of chariots rolled, three lakhs of elephants moved, six crores of horses, a vast number of mules and camels, and countless foot-soldiers marched.

In the meantime, Ravana's celebrated chariot bejewelled and loaded with celestial weapons, yoked to eight horses stood ready in effulgent splendour. He set forth amidst a flourish of trumpets, roll of tom-toms and tabors, blast of conches, and the wild clamour of the ogres. Surrounded by battalions of ogres, Ravana, with a most frightful aspect riding the chariot rushed to confront Rama. A mighty contest ensued. The monkeys were subjected to a hail of arrows, which they found irresistible. Wherever Ravana drove his chariot, the monkeys in that quarter could not withstand the mad assault of his arrows. They ran screaming.

Sugriva and the generals put all their energy into the fight. They hammered the demons with trees and rocks. A powerful giant, Virupaksha, riding an elephant, let out a terrible roar, and poured fierce arrows on Sugriva. The monkey king, seized with anger, tore up a tree and battered the elephant which under the stunning blow crumpled to the ground. Jumping down, as Virupaksha advanced, Sugriva hurled a huge rock on the enemy. Averting it the giant cut and destroyed Sugriva's armour. After a close encounter, Sugriva delivered a mighty blow on the demon, who fell to the ground. Likewise, many famed generals and commanders of Ravana were destroyed, together with their charioteers, by the monkey chief and the heroic Angada.

Seeing his powerful generals killed, a great rage seized Ravana, who stood determined for a showdown with Rama. Urging on his charioteer, he vowed he would do away with Rama and Lakshmana to avenge those killed and save his besieged kingdom. He would fell the 'tree' in the shape of Rama, whose principal boughs were Sugriva and the other monkey chiefs. With the chariot rattling with a terrific sound, Ravana drove rapidly towards Rama. The earth, with its rivers, mountains and forests, trembled.

Rama, accompanied by Lakshmana, took hold of his bow, and stretched it with immense force. Its twang made many demons fall. Meanwhile, Lakshmana let go his arrows that flew like tongues of fire. Ravana split them. Bypassing Lakshmana, he advanced to Rama. In the encounter, the two heroes pushed each other with the thrust of their arrows, describing circles of various kinds. The sky was filled with arrows which darted like lightning amidst dark clouds.

Resorting to conjuring tricks, Ravana shot missiles presided over by demoniac forces. He attacked with arrows carrying heads of tigers, lions, jackals, wolves, boars, alligators, falcons, vultures, serpents. In turn Rama let loose arrows some with heads bright as sun, crescent, comet, meteor, and others looking like flashes of lightning. Ravana's shafts, though nullified, killed the monkeys in thousands. From a missile presided over by Rudra and fashioned by the master conjurer, Maya, released by Ravana, issued on all sides flaming pikes, maces, clubs, mallets, nooses, and fierce thunderbolts. They lit up the sky. Rama split them.

Lakshmana tore Ravana's standard into pieces. He severed the head of the charioteer, and split asunder the bow of Ravana. Bouncing forward, Vibhishana struck down the horses with his mace. Leaping down from his chariot, Ravana displayed a violent rage against Vibhishana and flung at him a flaming javelin. With three shafts, Rama tore it asunder. The monkeys cheered riotously. Ravana, seizing a javelin, renowned for its infallibility flung it at Vibhishana; Lakshmana thwarted it with volleys of arrows. Facing Lakshmana, who rescued Vibhishana, Ravana flung violently the javelin designed by Maya which, possessing magical powers, hit the bosom of Lakshmana and threw him on the ground. Seeing Lakshmana in such predicament, Rama spoke to Hanuman: "I vow that before long the world would be rid of Ravana. He could escape no more than a serpent that had fallen under the gaze of Garuda. Let the three worlds see today the Ramahood of Rama. I shall accomplish a deed which all living beings, including the gods, shall recount."

Rama, who was stricken with sorrow at the state of Lakshmana, lamented: "Wives may be found, but not a brother like Lakshmana!" Susena consoled him. He addressed Hanuman: "Bring the four precious herbs 'visalyakarani', 'suvarnakarani', 'samjvakarani', and 'sandhani'. O, gallant one, you alone can do it, bounding with all speed to the Himalaya. Hanuman, with immeasurable velocity, repeated his feat, to bring the rare herbs. As Susena applied the herbs, Lakshmana rose to his feet, rid of pain. Rejoiced, Rama pressed him to his bosom. Hanuman duly restored the mountain crags.

The gods who wanted to see Ravana destroyed felt the combat was unequal, with Ravana seated in the chariot and Rama standing on the ground. Lord Indra ordered his charioteer, Matali, to take his chariot to Rama with the request that he be seated in it to fight Ravana.

Matali got ready the glorious chariot, wrought with gold, bearing a standard on a golden staff, yoked to splendid green horses. Descending, the divine charioteer stood in front of Rama. Matali submitted the chariot would bring victory to Rama. He presented to Rama Lord Indra's bow, as well as his armour aflame as fire. "Mounting the chariot, and with me as your charioteer, O, heroic prince, make short work of Ravana." Going round the chariot and saluting it, Rama ascended it.

Then occurred a marvellous duel between Rama and Ravana never before seen on the earth. A missile from Ravana turned into innumerable serpents with mouths blazing fire. Thus confronted, Rama discharged the missile presided over by Garuda, which, turning into golden eagles, devoured the snakes in a trice.

Ravana pierced Matali with a stream of shafts and felled his golden ensign. He struck the horses. Rama gave way to a fierce rage, filling all created beings with dread. Ominous portents occurred. Ravana seized by fear roared. He hurled darts powerful as thunderbolts. Rama pierced Ravana with many arrows, which made his limbs bleed profusely. He upbraided:

"The lord of Lanka, you have transgressed the bounds of morality, and you would go the way of Khara."

Asserting so, Rama got into a confident, joyous mood and covered Ravana with a shower of shafts. All the mystic missiles revealed themselves to the hero, who brimmed with martial ardour. Exposed to his attack, and struck with volleys of stones from the monkeys, Ravana got bewildered at heart. His mind confused, he lost dexterity in handling weapons, nor could he wield his bow. He saw the imminence of his death. His charioteer, seeing Ravana's plight, drove away in dismay.

Ravana, outraged, and his eyes bloodshot in anger, reproached his charioteer: "You acted according to your own choice. What for did you drive away my chariot, belittling me? Your action has sullied my valour and dignity." He ordered him to drive the chariot back to the battlefield.

The charioteer submitted his action was conceived in solicitude and affection, in an unpropitious situation. It was his duty. On command of Ravana, the charioteer drove the horses, making the chariot stand in an instant in front of Rama. This came to be a decisive encounter. Witnessing it, sage Agasthya, accompanied by the gods, approached Rama and said: "Hearken to the eternal secret. The encomium called Adityahridaya, that is installed in the heart of the orb of sun, is the source of blessing. Offer worship to the sun god, the source of light and all energy. That will enable you to conquer Ravana." The sage imparted the alleluia to Rama, and departed. Absorbing it with reverence, Rama worshipped the sun god, chanting the prayer, and experienced felicity. Highly exhilarated in mind, Rama stood, eager to engage Ravana.

Seeing Ravana, Rama spoke to Matali respectfully, "See Ravana daring forward recklessly, as if set on destroying himself. I need hardly advise you!" Hearing the courteous words, Matali directed the chariot on adroitly. Fearful omens appeared. Violent whirlwinds blew. Lanka looked wrapped in dusk. Thunderbolts fell on Ravana's army on all sides. The wind coursed unfavourably to him. Tears flowed from his horses. Ravana in grim chagrin saw disaster coming to him. As for Rama, he experienced joy. The heroic mood filled him.

The two armies poised for fight gazed in awe, wonder and ecstasy, standing motionless for a moment 'like a painting'! Then ensued an encounter between Ravana and Rama, without a parallel anywhere.

Ravana targeted the standard on Rama's chariot, but the arrows falling short crashed on the ground. An arrow from Rama's bow tore asunder Ravana's ensign. Fallen a prey to wrath, Ravana pierced Rama's horses. The heavenly steeds neither staggered nor reeled. Seeing their nonchalance, Ravana rained weapons including trees and mountain peaks, created through his magic. Rama, who fought calmly, sent arrows in hundreds and thousands. Ravana matched him by enveloping the sky with his shafts. The dazzling shower released continuously created, as it were, a new sky! All created beings gazed on the encounter with astonishment. The two charioteers driving the vehicles in circles, moving straight, darting and receding showed their marvellous skill. As Matali came under attack, Rama loosed twenty, thirty, sixty, hundreds and thousands of arrows on the opposing chariot. Ravana tormented Rama with maces and mallets. The fight was awe-inspiring. The globe, with the mountains and forests, experienced a tremor. The seven seas were thrown into agitation by the flight and clash of weapons. The celestials prayed, 'May Rama conquer Ravana!' Watching the struggle, they experienced thrill and exclaimed the struggle between Rama and Ravana could be likened only to the struggle between Rama and Ravana! There was never an equal to it.

Sending a shaft that looked like a serpent in agitation, Rama cut off a head of Ravana, resplendent with dazzling earrings. It fell on the ground. The three worlds witnessed the event with awe. Lo, a head, an exact replica of the one cut off, grew on Ravana's shoulders. Rama slashed that too, whereupon another sprouted in its place. Rama's shaft severed that too, and again another head manifested. Rama felled that as well. In this way, a hundred heads were struck off by Rama. And they came restored! A wonder of wonders, the sight thrilled and surprised all creation!

Rama became thoughtful. He wondered how his arrows, which made short work of Maricha, Khara, Viradha, Kabandha

and the invincible Bali, failed against Ravana! Rama now showered arrows on the breast of Ravana, who in turn tormented Rama with maces. The fight continued for entire days and nights, not ceasing even for a moment. Seeing no end, Matali addressed Rama: "How do you act as if you do not know, and as if I should refresh your memory? O gallant prince, discharge on him the mystic missile presided over by God Brahma. The hour of doom for Ravana as foretold by the gods has come."

Rama took hold of the weapon which sage Agasthya had, among other missiles, bestowed on him in the forest. Wind god sat over its feathers, fire god on its head; it was made of ether; Mandara and Meru mountains presided over its weight. Decked with gold and lovely feathers, the arrow emitted splendour and shone like the sun. Charging it with mystic spell, Rama placed it on his bow. The earth trembled. Stretching the bow full, Rama who felt highly exhilarated, loosed the arrow. Incapable of being resisted, the arrow landed on the chest of Ravana. It pierced his heart, taking the life out of the celebrated hero of overwhelming power and unique achievements. Its mission accomplished, the missile returned to Rama's quiver.

Ravana, dropped down from his chariot to the ground. The happening was incredible. Seeing it the rakshasas ran in all directions, being plagued by the monkeys. The battlefield resounded to the roar of jubilant victors.

The devas rained flowers in profusion. A fragrance sprang up wafting heavenly odours. The charanas sang. 'Well done', the gods hailed the deed for which they had been longing. Sugriva, Angada, Hanuman and other chiefs, and Vibhishana paid their homage to the princes. Lakshmana rejoiced at the fulfilment of his brother's mission. Rama, equanimous and steadfast as ever, stood glorious in the midst of the monkey forces.

Vibhishana lamented the death of his brother, who had

expelled him. "O, valiant one, my advice did not find favour with you, infatuated as you were. Neither your son, Indrajit, nor your minister, Prahasta, advised you properly or prized my warning. What with your valour, energy, and might, ability for asceticism, intelligence and accomplishments, which were never matched in battle even by the gods, you have been struck down by Rama's righteous anger."

Rama asked Vibhishana to perform the obsequies, due to his brother.

On hearing the news of Ravana's death, Mandodari lamented. His other consorts were stricken with grief. Seeing him lying in dust, they fell on him with tears flowing.

Mandodari was inconsolable. "O, younger brother of Kubera, you had become irresistible. I guess the Supreme Spirit, God Narayana, in the form of a man took away your life. The death of Khara at the hands of Rama at Janasthana should have warned you. Your passion for Sita, who is superior even to Arundhati, was foolish. I had admonished you. Surely, you have been consumed by the fire of Sita's virtue. I am undone; I shall grieve for numberless years."

Rama advised Vibhishana, who was in doubt, "Hostilities should end with death." Vibhishana did his duties with due ceremonies.

Having performed his tasks, Rama expressed joy, in the company of Lakshmana, Sugriva, and the monkey chiefs. Laying aside his bow and arrows and the divine armour gifted by Indra, he forsook his anger. He assumed a gentle demeanour. He respectfully saluted Matali, who thereupon departed with the chariot.

The celestial beings, who witnessed the destruction of Ravana and the matchless valour of Rama and the might of the monkeys, withdrew in their aerial cars.

Rama hugged Sugriva. He asked his brother to consecrate Vibhishana on the throne of Lanka. Lakshmana conducted the ceremony, with sea water brought expeditiously by the monkeys. Lanka rejoiced in the happy event.

Rama asked Hanuman to seek permission of king Vibhishana to proceed to the asoka grove and tell Sita the events, and to return with her message. Anjaneya found Sita sitting cheerless at the foot of the tree. He stood before her motionless, bent low

in reverence. Looking at him, and recognizing him, Sita rejoiced. Hanuman communicated Rama's message. "Rama is doing well, along with Lakshmana and Sugriva. Assisted by Vibhishana and the monkeys, he has accomplished his purpose. He has enquired of your welfare. O, godlike lady, Rama has scored his victory by virtue of your devotion to your husband." He informed her that Vibhishana, who had become the king, would come to pay his respect to her.

Sita, whose countenance became bright, remained tongue-tied, for a little time, overwhelmed by joy. She said, "I can think of nothing on earth or in the three worlds which matches your act of merit in communicating this most agreeable news to me. I do not find anything worthy to bestow on you." Hanuman said: "You alone can utter such precious words." Sita praised him for his strength, valour, scriptural knowledge, vigour, prowess, superb skill, spirit, forbearance, firmness, stability, and modesty. "Your speech is endowed with mellifluence and has all excellences."

Hanuman stood unembarrassed. Truly tactful and gifted with subtle humour, Hanuman probed: "Shall I destroy with my fists the demonesses who, keeping guard over you, harassed you?"

Sita answered, "O, jewel among monkeys, my own error brought my suffering. I condone the acts of the slaves. A bear said to a tiger, 'a superior one forgives faults'. The principle of not returning evil for evil must be redeemed at all cost. The virtuous carry good conduct as their ornament." Albeit admonished gently, Hanuman was happy in his heart. He asked for a message to be taken to Rama. Sita gave her message: "I long to see my lord, who is fond of his devotees."

"You shall this day see Rama," assured Hanuman, seeing her eyes bedimmed with tears.

On receiving the message, Rama asked Vibhishana to bring Sita. The king entered the asoka grove, brought Sita duly robed and adorned with rare jewels in a brilliant palanquin to Rama's presence. He thought he would disperse the crowd of monkeys and demons, but Rama mildly reproached: "Neither apartments nor costumes nor a protective wall constitute a veil for a woman. Her character alone is her shield. There is no objection to her appearing, particularly in my presence. Let the monkeys see my spouse, the princess of Videha. Let her walk on foot."

Precious words!

Vibhishana reverently conducted Sita to Rama's presence. She stood facing Rama. The sight of her lord dispelled her fatigue. Rama remained thoughtful over Sita having lived in Lanka for a year. Fire god, the supreme purifier, appeared in his glorious bodily form and proclaimed Sita's purity and blemishlessness. Accepting the averment, Rama received Sita. The gods witnessed the event with extreme joy.

On the advice of God Siva, Rama and Lakshmana paid their homage to the soul of their father, Dasaratha, who appeared in an ethereal form. Dasaratha blessed them. He blessed Sita. Rama begged him: "Be gracious to Kaikeyi. You had said, 'I disown you with your son, Bharata'. May that curse not fall on mother Kaikeyi and her son."

Dasaratha said, 'So be it'. Clothed in splendour and filled with joy, the king ascended to heaven.

Lord Indra appeared and enquired if Rama had any wish to fulfil. Rama desired to see the monkeys, who fell dead for his sake, to come back to life. At the command of the Lord of heaven, all the monkeys rose as though having slept. They exulted in Rama's victory.

Seeing Rama having fully accomplished his purpose, the gods eulogized him.

King Vibhishana invited Rama to relax for a while amidst the comforts of Lanka. Rama for his part reminded that Bharata, who had been practising austerities on his account, was waiting. Therefore, he along with Lakshmana and Sita needed to reach Ayodhya without loss of time. Vibhishana said he would enable Rama to reach Ayodhya in a day. He invoked the aerial car, Pushpaka. It arrived. Decorated with gold and gems, shining like silver, unassailable and swift as thought, the chariot stood ready.

Rama thoughtfully asked Vibhishana to honour the monkeys, without exception, who did their task. As Rama, along with Sita and Lakshmana stood to bid adieu, Vibhishana, Sugriva, and the monkey chiefs expressed a desire to accompany him to see the coronation in Ayodhya. Rama agreed with genuine delight.

Pushpaka, which had the image of a swan, flew through the air. Flying to Ayodhya, Rama showed to Sita Lanka built by Viswakarma perched on a summit of the Trikuta mountain, the field of battle, the spots where Kumbhakarna, Indrajit and Ravana fought and were killed. Sita saw the scenes of the exploits of Hanuman, Sugriva, Angada and other monkey chiefs.

Sita saw the sea shore, where after crossing the sea, the army spent a night on the sethu built by the monkeys. She looked with amazement. Sita saw the turbulent ocean, which was crossed by Hanuman! Rama pointed to the spot where Vibhishana met him for refuge.

Pushpaka flew over Kishkindha, where Rama killed Bali. Seeing Kishkindha, Sita said she wished to reach Ayodhya accompanied by Ruma, consort of Sugriva, the noble Tara, as well as the wives of the other monkey chiefs. Sugriva agreed to the thoughtful suggestion. Pushpaka landed. Advised by Sugriva, Tara acknowledged the kindly act of Sita and felt happy to go to Ayodhya to see Rama's entry into the city and his coronation. Along with others, Tara entered Pushpaka.

The aerial car flew over the Pampa lake, over the mountain, where Sugriva first met Rama, over Janasthana where Rama disposed of Khara. Sita saw the hermitage from where she was taken away by Ravana, and Chitrakoot where Bharata had met Rama. Further on, Sita saw the delightful Yamuna hemmed in with lovely woods, the river Ganga, Sringaverapura where lived Guha, and the Sarayu lined with holy spots of sacrifices.

The city of Ayodhya came into view, to which Rama and Sita made reverential salutations.

Descending, the Pushpaka landed at the hermitage of sage Bharadwaja. Rama, who on that day completed fourteen years of his exile, received the blessings of the sage. He told Rama that wearing matted hair and placing Rama's wooden sandals in front of him, Bharata waited for his return. He should go to Ayodhya the next day.

As Rama proceeded to Ayodhya, the trees on the way burst into blossom with flowing honey, and bore fruits. On reaching the outskirts of Ayodhya, the monkeys feasted on the fruits.

Gazing with joy on Ayodhya, Rama asked Maruthi to go to Sringaverapura and communicate his welfare to Guha. He would have news about Bharata, who should be told of his return with

Sita and Lakshmana, accompanied by Vibhishana and Sugriva. Rama should receive Bharata's reactions.

Hanuman sprang forward, and crossing the confluence of the Yamuna and the Ganga (Prayag), he gave the message of Rama's return to Guha. Proceeding, Hanuman came across the waters of the rivers Valukim, Vamdhini and Gomati and saw the jungle growing in the Kosala kingdom. At Nandigrama with its trees in blossom, he saw Bharata emaciated, dwelling in a hermitage, wearing matted locks, with the bark of trees and the skin of a black antelope wrapped around his waist. He was afflicted through separation from Rama. He subsisted on fruits and roots, and was engaged in austerities. He resembled a rishi, ruling the earth, with Rama's wooden sandals in front of him. He was attended by upright ministers. Indeed the citizens themselves had abstained from too much pleasures seeing the prince's noble conduct.

Hanuman, with his arms joined, addressed Bharata: "Rama, for whom you are grieving, has enquired of your welfare. Give up your grief, I bring you the news that you will be united with Rama in a short while. He returns, with Lakshmana and Sita, having killed Ravana."

The news filled Bharata with calm ecstasy and bliss. He sank to the ground and fainted in happiness. Rising to his feet, Bharata embraced Hanuman and, with tears, said: "Whether you are a god or human being, you have come here through compassion. Tell me the whole truth."

Anjaneya told Bharata the story of Rama and his life in Chitrakoot, after Bharata had returned to Ayodhya, in the Dandaka forest, at Panchavati, abduction of Sita by Ravana, the killing of Bali and the events that followed until his victory.

He said Bharata would be able to see Rama who stayed with sage Bharadwaja.

Hearing the most heartening news, Bharata considered himself blessed. True to his rectitude, he commanded men of virtue to offer worship to their family deities, and in temples. He desired the bards, well versed in legends and cosmogony, the queen mothers, army men with their spouses, and others to proceed for the darshan of Rama.

Ayodhya thus prepared to receive the returning hero. The tract leading to Nandigrama was sprinkled with water. The streets were decorated with flags and flowers. Satrughna supervised the arrangements. The ministers arrived with adorned elephants. Eminent warriors on elephants, horses and in chariots and a large number of foot-soldiers followed.

Kausalya, Sumitra and Kaikeyi seated on palanquins travelled to Nandigrama.

Placing Rama's wooden sandals adorned with garlands on his head, Bharata accompanied by counsellors, Brahmanas, leaders of guilds of traders, and artisans, clad in ascetics robes, greeted Rama's arrival. Conches blew, drums sounded. The poet said the entire Ayodhya had reached Nandigrama!

Hanuman pointed to the flying divine car, and to the army of monkeys as it advanced, raising a cloud of dust. Pushpaka landed. The people beheld Rama seated in it, like 'the moon in the sky', Sita and Lakshmana, in the company of Vibhishana and Sugriva. Standing on the ground with joined palms, Bharata offered worship to Rama, from afar, with sprinkling of water. Bent low, Bharata saluted his brother who stood in the car. Descending on the earth, Rama embraced Bharata and placed him in his lap. Bharata embraced Lakshmana. He saluted Sita. He made obeisance to Sugriva, Vibhishana, as also the monkey chiefs, who had assumed human semblance. He told Sugriva with affection: "You are a fifth brother to us."

Taking the wooden sandals, which he had worshipped,

Bharata himself placed them below the feet of Rama. With joined palms, he said, "Here is your kingdom, held in trust so far, rendered back to you. My prayer stands consummated in your coming back to Ayodhya. Your exchequer, storehouses, palaces, and army have grown ten-fold by virtue of your moral force." Seeing Bharata's selfless conduct, the monkeys and their chiefs shed tears in admiration.

Rama, along with the monkeys, went to the hermitage of Bharata. Rama, standing on the ground, addressed the aerial car, which had been seized from Kubera by Ravana, "Let thee be gone to Kubera. I grant you leave to depart." Pushpaka thereupon rose into the sky and flew back to its original abode.

After touching sage Vasishta's feet, Rama sat by his side. Sumantra brought the chariot. Rama and Sita, Tara and the consorts of Sugriva ascended it, which drove to the city. Bharata himself took the reins of the horses. Satrughna held the parasol, and Lakshmana and Vibhishana fanned. Sugriva rode a mighty elephant, Satrumjaya, and the monkeys rode on innumerable elephants. Accompanied by blasts of conches, roll of drums, and shouts of joy, and surrounded by the ministers, the priests, the citizens and the monkeys, Rama entered the city. Musicians singing festive songs, citizens carrying grains of rice and sweets, Brahmanas and cows marched in front. The people raised aloft pennons on their dwellings. Rama, Sita, Lakshmana and Bharata reached the abode of their father in a mood of spontaneous affection and reverence. Kausalya, Sumitra and Kaikeyi, who had reached earlier, greeted them in the joy of reunion.

Preparations for the coronation in Ayodhya began, and went on briskly under the guidance of the arch-priest, Vasishta, assisted by the sages, Vamana, Jabali, Kasyapa, Katyayana, Suyajna, Gautama and Vijaya and others. Commanded by king Sugriva, the heroic Jambavan, Hanuman, Gavaya and Rishabha brought in golden pails waters from the four seas, and other simians from five hundred sacred rivers. Vasishta seated Rama on the throne made of precious stones, with Sita on his side. The sages caused the waters, as also fragrant waters and sap of rare medicinal herbs to be sprinkled on Rama. They placed on Rama the crown studded with gorgeous gems, and the rich jewellery, which were worn by Vaivaswata Manu and by the succession of kings in the lineage. Satrughna held the parasol, Sugriva and Vibhishana the white whisks.

Prompted by Lord Indra, wind god presented to Rama a garland of a hundred gold lotuses and also a pearl necklace which Rama duly placed on Sita. Unclasping the necklace conferred on her, Sita, her face glowing in pride and affection, looked at Hanuman, and cast a glance at Rama who said: "Gladly bestow it on Anjaneya with whom you are pleased." Forthwith,

Sita conferred it on Maruthi who shone 'like a peak silvered by an aureole of moonbeams'. Rama honoured the chiefs and the monkeys suitably.

Rama conferred on Sugriva a heavenly garland of gold shining with the brilliance of sun's rays, and on Angada, a pair of armlets made of cat's-eye gems.

The gandharvas sang beautifully, and the celestial nymphs danced. As the gods, sages, Brahmanas, traders, artisans, citizens and the monkeys looked on the great event, flowers rained. The whole nature glowed. The earth, redeemed by Rama's godly deeds culminating in his succession, gaining freshness and beauty, lay covered with crops, and the trees standing firmly on the ground flowered and fruited emitting fragrance. The clouds rained. Joy filled all creation on the festal occasion!

Rama gave away horses, cows with calves, raiments and ornaments and desired objects.

Having assumed the rulership of the kingdom, Rama spoke to Lakshmana, "Rule with me, O knower of what is right, this earth which was protected by the former kings. Installed as prince regent bear you, like me, the burden which was borne by our forbears." Soumitri politely declined. Thereupon Rama consecrated Bharata as prince regent.

The coronation ceremonies over, Sugriva, Ruma, Tara and the other ladies, the monkey chiefs returned to Kishkindha. Vibhishana went back to Lanka.

Rama's rule began. The Brahmanas, Kshatriyas and other sections of the citizens performed their duties ardently, and worked for the prosperity of the kingdom. The people remained free, rid of fear, devoted to ethical conduct. One name remained constantly on their lips—Rama.

UTTARA KANDA
Epilogue

Bharata told Rama, "It is but a little over a month since you accepted the sceptre of rulership. The people have become free of travails. The citizens in the towns and the country say such rulership should last for long."

Rama, after performing his religious rites and kingly duties, spent the time with Sita in the beautiful royal garden. They gave delight to each other.

Rama, who saw auspicious signs of motherhood on Sita, said to her, "O, lovely lady, which desire of yours should be fulfilled?" Sita responded: "My wish is to visit the penance-groves of the sages in the forest who live on roots and fruits. I long to spend at least a night at their feet." Rama said: "So be it, and tomorrow."

The king had in his court witty narrators who brought stories, talks on the affairs of the state gathered from the people. Rama addressed them: "Tell me without fear what the people talk about the king, Sita, about my brothers, and my mothers." One among the narrators, Bhadra said, with folded hands: "While the people laud your glorious deeds, they say Rama took back into his house Sita who was carried away by Ravana and who lived in Lanka for a year. She escaped censure! Such conduct of our wives shall have to be suffered by us, since whatever the king does, the subjects follow."

Rama sent for his brothers. His face withered, he shared with them the story he had heard. "Fire god declared Sita to be pure. My conscience bears testimony to her nobility yet the censure of the people pains my heart. I dread infamy even as the gods do. I do not see a greater misfortune, O, brothers!"

The king ordered Lakshmana, "Taking Sita, leave her near sage Valmiki's ashrama. She had said: 'I wish to behold the penance-groves in the forest'. I fulfil her heart's desire." His command should be carried out without the least resistance.

Lakshmana told Sita in the palace: "You shall be taken to the forest hermitage immediately at your lord's bidding." Sita, who was highly pleased, gathered precious garments and gems to be gifted to the spouses of the ascetics.

Sumantra drove the chariot yoked to the best horses. Seated in it, Sita told Lakshmana: "I see ill-omens in abundance. May all be well with your brother, and welfare be with mothers."

"All is well," Lakshmana said laconically and fell silent. He took Sita across the Ganga. Urged by her, Lakshmana with an agitated mind said she was to be abandoned for reason of censure by the people! Sita swooned away. Waking, she said: "This mortal frame of mine was indeed created for sorrow, O, Lakshmana! I cannot give up my life, for the royal family of my lord will be broken." Lakshmana, who had never looked on Sita's face, bowed, his head touching the earth, and went round her crying uncontrollably. He left.

Valmiki, knowing the happening through his ascetic power, took Sita into his hermitage. The sage said to her: "I have perceived you to be free from guilt. Be composed as if you are entering your own home, child." Female ascetics looked after her.

Twin sons were born to Sita. The sage named them, Kusa, the elder, Lava, the younger. The children grew into dazzling boyhood, rich in beauty, bravery and prowess.

Valmiki taught them Rama's story. They learned it in the poetic and musical measure as originally composed by him.

Meanwhile, Rama performed the Aswamedha sacrifice. Valmiki took Kusa and Lava to the yaga. He told his cheerful pupils: "Go and sing Rama's story in the huts of the sages, in the dwellings of the Brahmanas, in the byways and highways, in the houses of the invited ones. Sing at the entrance of the

195

apartment of Rama, and where the ritual is being performed."

That was in the evening. In the morning, the children having bathed and made offerings to fire, sang as instructed by the sage. Rama heard the song in rapture. The boys sang the poem in a 'sweet voice and most joyfully' before the large assembly of invited rulers, ascetics, learned Brahmanas, citizens and experts in music, to the accompaniment of lutes. Amazement filled the listeners. On the king's enquiry, the boys said they were taught by the venerable sage, Valmiki, 'keeping in mind your deeds'! For many days the assembly heard the wonderful recital by the precocious pair. Rama understood they were the sons of Sita!

Rama sent an envoy to Valmiki. He arrived. The sage declared: "Kusa and Lava are indeed your sons, difficult to conquer. I have deemed Sita to be guiltless. The sinless, looking upon her husband as a god, shall affirm."

Rama said: "The censure by folks is great, therefore, I forsook Sita, although knowing she was sinless. I know Kusa and Lava are my sons. May my love for Maithili, the pure one, be proclaimed. Maithili's avowal will be purification for me also."

Meanwhile, Sita, who had followed Valmiki, said with folded hands and downcast eyes: "I have not contemplated anyone other than the scion of Raghu. As I worship Rama in mind, speech and action, and as I have spoken the truth, O, earth goddess, grant me space to enter!" As she was talking, the earth opened up and engulfed Vaidehi! The vast concourse that looked on the event was lost in sorrow and wonderment.

Rama was filled with intense agony, and anger willing to churn up the earth. In the presence of God Brahma and other gods who knew Rama and Sita were inseparably one ever, Rama, the best of the Raghu race, becalmed himself.

During his long rule Rama performed many more Aswamedha yagas at which an image of Sita in gold occupied the queen's place.

196

SELECT GLOSSARY

Agasthya great sage, son of Mitra and Varuna by Urvasi, husband of Lopamudra, presented Vishnu's bow, among other divine weapons, to Rama.

Ahalya consort of rishi Gautama, who seeing loss of her chastity through Indra's deceit cursed her to remain frozen until Rama's feet touched her.

Anasuya wife of sage Atri, a mind-born son of Brahma, famous for her fidelity.

Ansuman son of Asamanja, and grandson of king Sagara, ancestors of Rama.

Aruna son of Kasyapa and Vinata, brother of Garuda, father of Sampathi and Jatayu.

Arundhati wife of Vasishta, epitome of wifely devotion.

Aswamedha horse-sacrifice performed by a monarch to establish his supremacy.

Aswapati king of Kekaya, Kaikeyi's father.

Atiratha a car-hero who can fight alone many a Maharatha, a great warrior or charioteer, defending himself, his charioteer and horses.

Bhagiratha son of Dilipa of the solar dynasty, ancestor of Rama, who through untiring effort brought the Ganga to the earth and washed away the sins of his 60,000 uncles, sons of Sagara and Sumati, who were cursed by sage Kapila, a manifestation of Vishnu, hence the name Bhagirathi for the Ganga.

Bhargava (lit.) who descended from the line of Bhrigu, Parasurama, son of Jamadagni and Renuka.

Dundubhi buffalo-demon, brother of Mayavi, both killed by king Bali in encounter.

Dushana a brother of Surpanakha, Khara, and half-brother of Ravana.

Guha chief of a nishada tribe, Rama's friend, who ruled from Sringaverapura near Ayodhya.

Ikshwaku ancestor of Rama, son of Vaivaswata Manu.

Jahnu a sage who drank up the waters of the Ganga and released her through his ears, hence the name Jahnavi for the river.

Jambavan mighty bear in Sugriva's simian army, who had circled the earth to proclaim the Vamana incarnation of Vishnu.

Janaka family name for Mithila kings; Siradhwaja, father of Sita.

Kabandha a gandharva under a curse, a massive giant released by Rama.

Karthaveerarjuna thousand-armed king of the Hehayas, who ruled from Mahishmati, killed by Parasurama.

Kasyapa an eminent sage, a grandson of Brahma.

Khara son of Visrava and brother of Surpanakha and half-brother of Ravana who, along with his enormous horde, was killed by Rama at Janasthana.

Kubera son of Visrava, hence also Vaisravana, and half-brother of Ravana, lord of riches.

Kumbhakarna (lit.) pot-ear, son of Visrava, brother of Ravana, who got from Brahma the boon of 'eternal sleep', enormous in form, killed by Rama.

Kusadhwaja king Janaka's younger brother, father of Mandavi, Srutakirti, wives of Bharata, Satrughna.

Lanka-Sri the embodied glory of Lanka, an ogress at its gates whom Hanuman smote and freed from a curse.

Malyavan   maternal grandfather of Ravana.

Mandodari   incarnation of apsara Madhura, daughter of Maya, wife of Ravana, mother of Indrajit and Aksha.

Manthara   Kaikeyi's hunchback maid, who instigated her to send Rama into exile.

Maricha   son of Sunda and Tataka, who in the guise of a golden deer lured Rama away from Sita in Panchavati.

Meghanada (lit.)   sound of clouds, another name for Indrajit, so called for conquering Indra.

Nahusha   ancestor of Rama, father of Yayati.

Nala   a heroic monkey, son of Viswakarma, and architect of the bridge to Lanka, hence 'Nala-sethu'.

Nila   a prominent monkey general in Sugriva's army.

Punjikasthala   daughter of Varuna, nymph in heaven, who cursed Ravana.

Pulastya   born of Brahma, an eminent sage, progenitor of Visrava, Ravana's father.

Raghu   son of Kakutasta, through whom and others, the lineage descended to Aja, Dasaratha; Raghuvamsa after his name.

Rambha   a beautiful apsara who, violated, cursed Ravana.

Rishyamuka hill   close to Pampa lake, resorted to by Sugriva in exile, forbidden to Bali.

Sabari   an aged female ascetic, who attained salvation when Rama visited her.

Sarabhanga   a sage in the Dandaka forest, who was visited by Rama.

Satananda   son of Ahalya and Gautama, family priest of Janaka.

Simhika   ogress who clutched flying Hanuman's shadow from below and was killed by him.

Subahu   son of Tataka, accomplice of Maricha.

Sunda   asura, brother of Upasunda, fought and killed each other to possess apsara Tilottama.

Surasa   mother of serpents, as giantess with a wide, hungry mouth waylaid Hanuman in his flight to Lanka, who in a dimunitive form emerged through her ear, and was blessed.

Sutikshna   a hermit who advised Rama to visit places and to whom Rama returned.

Swayamprabha   of rare asceticism who helped the monkey contingent to emerge from a deep cave in the forest where they got confused, and guided them to go in the southern direction; she saw Rama and attained liberation.

Tara   consort of Bali, famed for her beauty, poise and tact.

Trijata   a rakshasi who guarded Sita in Lanka and had sympathy for her.

Vaivaswata Manu   seventh Manu, son of Vivaswan, progenitor of the solar dynasty.

Vedavati   apsara who was sought to be molested by Ravana, reborn as Sita.

Vidyujjihva   a master conjurer employed by Ravana who created illusion of Rama having been killed to demoralise Sita.

Viradha   gandharva Tumburu cursed to be a demon, regained his old form as Rama and Lakshmana liberated him.

Viswamitra   son of Gadhi, born as a Kshatriya, later became a celebrated royal sage whose sacrifice Rama protected and who gave Rama many celestial missiles; Kousika, another name for the sage.

*In respect of a few entries, multiple versions obtain.

"There is one descended in the line of Ikshwaku, and known by the name of Rama. He has fully controlled his mind, is very powerful, radiant and resolute and has brought his senses under control...He knows the secret of virtue, and is true to his promise and intent on the good of the people. He is illustrious, full of wisdom, pure in his dealings, a man of self-control and concentrated mind. He is a supporter of the creation, affluent, the slayer of enemies, a protector of living beings and a staunch defender of faith. He is a vindicator of his own virtue and the protector of his own people. He knows the truth of the Vedas and the sciences auxiliary to them...He knows the meaning of all scriptures. He is always 'sought by the righteous even as the ocean is by the rivers'. He is noble, nay, alike to all and always wears a pleasing countenance. He is endowed with all excellences...He vies with the ocean in profundity and compares with the Himalaya in point of firmness...He who reads this sacred narration of Rama, which is capable of purifying the mind, and wiping out sins, and is treated on a par with the Vedas, is completely absolved from all sins. Reading this narrative centring round Rama...a man shall on departing from this world be honoured in heaven."

—Sage Narada